THE GREAT FATHERLAND WAR

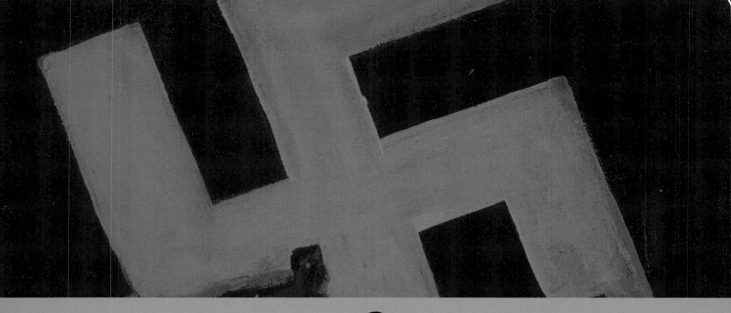

THE GREAT FATHERLAND WAR

WAR

THE RISE AND FALL OF THE SOVIET UNION

TED GOTTFRIED

ILLUSTRATED BY MELANIE REIM

TWENTY-FIRST CENTURY BOOKS
BROOKFIELD, CONNECTICUT

For my friend,
Daniel Mark Gottfried,
the best of sons.
I'll drink to that.

Acknowledgments
I am grateful to personnel of the New York Central Research Library, the Mid-Manhattan Library, the Society Library in New York, and the Queensboro Public Library for aid in gathering material for this book. Also, gratitude and much love to my wife, Harriet Gottfried, who—as always—read and critiqued this book. Her help was invaluable, but any shortcomings in the work are mine alone.

Ted Gottfried

Photographs courtesy of Getty Images/Hulton/Archive: pp. 15, 19, 25, 32, 35, 97, 107; AP/Wide World Photos: pp. 43, 53, 67; Süddeutscher Verlag Bilderdienst: p. 76; National Archives: p. 85. Map by Joe LeMonnier.

Library of Congress Cataloging-in-Publication Data
Gottfried, Ted.
The Great Fatherland War : the Soviet Union in World War II / Ted Gottfried; illustrations by Melanie Reim.
 p. cm. — (The rise and fall of the Soviet Union)
Summary: Discusses the Soviet Union's involvement in World War II, from their non-agression pact with Germany to their subsequent invasion and eventual defeat, highlighting the hardships endured by the Soviet people during the war years.
Includes bibliographical references and index.
ISBN 0-7613-2559-X (lib. bdg,)
1. World War, 1939-1945—Soviet Union—Juvenile literature. 2. World War, 1939-1945—Destruction and pillage—Soviet Union. [1. World War, 1939-1945—Soviet Union. 2. Soviet Union—History—1939-1945.] I. Reim, Melanie K., ill. II. Title.
D764 .G659 2003   940.53'47—dc21   2002005328
            GOT

Published by Twenty-First Century Books
A Division of The Millbrook Press, Inc.
2 Old New Milford Road
Brookfield, Connecticut 06804
www.millbrookpress.com

17727

CONTENTS

OCEAN

BERING SEA

EAST SIBERIAN SEA

LAPTEV SEA

Anadyr

Ambarchik

Nizhnekolymsk

Kolyma R.

Nordvik

Magadan

Kamchatka
Peninsula

Petropavlosk

Lena R.

Okhotsk

SEA OF
OKHOTSK

Dudinka

Arctic Circle

SIBERIA

Yakutsk

Viluisk

Mangazeia

Turukhansk

Tura

Sakhalin
Island

Yenisey R.

Aldan

Nikolaevsk

Trans-Siberian Railway,
completed in 1917

Angara R.

Amur R.

OCIALIST REPUBLICS

Khabarovsk

Tomsk

Krasnoyarsk

Bratsk

Lake
Baikal

Kara

JAPAN

Cheremkhovo
Irkutsk

Nerchinsk

Oka R.

MANCHURIA

SEA
OF
JAPAN

Vladivostok

MONGOLIA

GERMAN FORCES
IN THE
SOVIET UNION,
WORLD WAR II

KOREA

········· Farthest advance
of German forces

| 0 | 300 miles |

| 0 | 450 kilometers |

CHINA

PREFACE

To Americans it was World War II, a war fought on three continents — Europe, Asia, and Africa — and a host of islands large and small, a war fought on vast oceans and strategic seas, and in the skies over land and water. Although Pearl Harbor and the Hawaiian Islands, territories of the United States, were bombed by the Japanese, no battles were fought in the continental United States. When it came to physical danger, the home front was far from the battle zones.

The U.S. home front viewed the war in terms of those zones. There was the Pacific, Asia, North Africa, Italy, and later France, Belgium, and Germany. In addition, there was the Russian front, which is how Americans often referred to it. It was far away, and while the people of the Union of Soviet Socialist Republics (USSR) were our allies, they were Communists. They were fighting the Nazis, but only a short while before they had joined with them in the conquest of Poland. Americans understood that the battles in the Soviet Union were important, but our own boys were fighting and dying in a score of other places in World War II. None were involved in the struggles on the so-called Russian front.

Naturally, the people of the USSR regarded it differently. It was not World War II to them. It was the Great Fatherland War. Eleven million Soviet soldiers died on the battlefield. The enemy — the Germans and their allies — lost only three million. In all of World War II, the United States had only 405,000 fatalities, and Great Britain had only 375,000.[1]

Soviet civilian casualties added to the death toll. Geoffrey Hosking, professor of Russian History at the University of London, estimates that altogether "some 20–25 million Soviet citizens died premature deaths between 1941 and 1945." He points out that this was more lives than had been lost by any nation in any war in history.[2] Some died in battle, some were killed as prisoners of the Germans, some starved to death, some froze, and some were worked to death. In one way or another, all were casualties of the Great Fatherland War.

What follows is an account of that conflict. It is a saga of humanity at its very worst—and at its very best. It is a record of leadership and incompetence, patriotism and betrayal, bravery and cowardice, sacrifice and selfishness, hardship and brutality. Such were the ingredients of the Great Fatherland War.

CHAPTER
ONE

THE WEHRMACHT
INVASION

> They had no prepared schemes on which to fall back in event of a sudden Nazi attack because Stalin had decreed that there would be no Nazi attack. If a dictator decrees that there will be no attack, an officer who prepares for one is liable to execution as a traitor.
>
> Historian and *New York Times* foreign correspondent Harrison Salisbury describes the effect of Joseph Stalin's obstinacy on the eve of the Nazi invasion of the Soviet Union.

It was sunrise on a Sunday morning in June, and the waters of Leningrad Harbor were shimmering with reflected yellows, oranges, and reds. The *Rukhno*, a small, elegant Estonian passenger steamer, had just taken Fyodor Trofimov, a harbor pilot, on board. It was his job to steer the luxury vessel through the channel to the open sea where the captain would take over the helm. Guiding the ship slowly and carefully, Trofimov noticed the glitter of the rising sun on the domes and cupolas of Leningrad. The sunlight spread out over the white sailboats anchored in the harbor. The morning was still young, and the scene was hushed and peaceful.

ABANDON SHIP!

The quiet—the peace—was shattered by a sudden, ear-shattering explosion. Trofimov was tossed like a straw in the wind to the far side of the bridge and slammed against the bulkhead. Dazed, he picked himself up to find blood running down the side of his head. Half deafened by the explosion, he dimly heard cries of *Abandon ship!* and the roar of steam escaping from the hold. The *Rukhno* was beginning to list.

It would be only a matter of time before the ship sank. If it went down where it now was, in mid-channel, Leningrad Harbor would be completely blocked. Leningrad was a major port, and its more than three million citizens were heavily dependent on the food shipments that passed through the harbor. The blocked channel would be a disaster.

Trofimov, still dazed, pulled himself back to the helm. At first the steering mechanism did not respond. Then, slowly, the *Rukhno* began to turn. It nosed toward the bank of the channel. At the same time, it continued sinking and moved more and more slowly. When the water reached the bridge, Trofimov leaped from the ship. As he was being pulled into a lifeboat by rescuers he watched the *Rukhno* go down next to the bank, leaving the channel clear. A moment later Trofimov learned from his rescuers that the German army had invaded, and the Soviet Union was at war. The date was June 22, 1941.

TARGET: LENINGRAD

Leningrad was the second most important city in the Union of Soviet Socialist Republics after Moscow, the capital. Before the Bolshevik Revolution, Leningrad had been called St. Petersburg and served as the capital of Imperial Tsarist Russia. During World War I, the name was changed to Petrograd, and later to Leningrad in honor of Vladimir Lenin, the first head of the Soviet nation. Since the collapse of the Soviet Union in August 1991, the city has again been called St. Petersburg. Throughout World War II, however, it was still known as Leningrad.

Situated in the northwestern corner of the USSR, Leningrad was perhaps the most strategically located Soviet city in the war. It was a port city at the mouth of the Neva River on the Gulf of Finland, the only access the USSR had to the Baltic Sea. It was about 25 miles from Lake Ladoga, the largest lake in Europe, with an area of 6,826 square miles.

Leningrad is a cold city, covered by snow an average of 132 days a year. Both the Neva River and Lake Ladoga are frozen over from mid-November through mid-April. The winter nights are very long, but the half-light of early summer results in the so-called white nights for which Leningrad is renowned.[1]

In 1941, Leningrad was a beautiful city, celebrated for its Winter Palace and for the domes and steeples of its architecture. Surrounded by sandy beaches and green forests, it nevertheless produced 11 percent of the industrial output of the USSR at that time. This was another reason why it was a primary target of the German army. By September 1941 the Wehrmacht (German army) had reached the outskirts of the city and had cut off all of Leningrad's communications with the rest of the Soviet Union.

DOUBLE DOUBLE CROSSES

The Soviet Union was the largest country in the world at the time of the German invasion in World War II. It covered roughly eight and a half million square miles, approximately one sixth of the land surface of the Earth. Spanning the two continents of Europe and Asia, the USSR stretched from the Baltic Sea, Barents Sea, and Bering Strait in the north, to Iran, Afghanistan, China, Mongolia, and Korea in the south; from the borders of German-occupied Poland, Hungary, and Romania and the Black Sea in the west, and to the Bering Sea and the Sea of Japan in the east. It was made up of fifteen Soviet republics with a total population in excess of 200 million people.

Prior to the attack on the USSR, under the terms of a pact between Nazi Germany and the Soviet Union, the two countries had invaded Poland. The Soviets had occupied an area of 76,500 square miles with a population of 12.8 million Polish citizens. The area and its people had been split up between two Soviet republics—Byelorussia and the Ukraine—and communized according to doctrines laid down by the Soviet dictator, Joseph Stalin. He had also ordered the occupation of the nations of Latvia, Lithuania, and Estonia. A brief war against Finland had ended in 1940 with a takeover of strategic Finnish territory by the Soviets.

All of the Soviet conquests were related to its August 1939 nonaggression agreement with Nazi Germany. It was an agreement that shocked the world. Adolf Hitler, the dictator of Germany, had been the architect of the Anti-Comintern Pact signed with Japan in November 1936, and with Italy a year later. The pact sealed an alliance to fight communism—specifically,

Vyacheslav Molotov, Russian foreign minister, signs the 1939 nonaggression pact between Soviet Russia and Germany, while his German counterpart Joachim von Ribbentrop (left) and Joseph Stalin (center) look on.

the spread of communism by the Third International headquartered in Moscow. Germany's 1939 agreement with Russia, resulting in the conquest and division of Poland between the two countries, violated the Anti-Comintern Pact. It also contradicted Hitler's vows over many years to destroy Soviet communism.

Stalin had provided armaments and manpower to fight fascism and German Nazi warplanes in Spain. He had supported German Communists against the Nazi party. He had pledged to fight Nazi aggression in Eastern Europe, specifically Poland. He betrayed his record and went back on his word when he signed the 1939 pact with Hitler. Now, in 1941, the question was: Why should he be surprised that the Nazis were again betraying an ally and invading his country?

INEVITABLY, OR SOONER?

As early as June 1940, Prime Minister Winston Churchill of Great Britain had sent Stalin a message that he had information that Germany was mobilizing to attack Russia. In February 1941, Stalin had been alerted by Soviet military intelligence that the German High Command was "pursuing systematic preparations for a war against the Soviet Union."[2] In early March a Soviet secret agent warned that the Germans were planning an attack, and subsequently gave the exact date for the invasion: June 22, 1941. On March 20, Stalin was informed of the objectives of the three major German army groups slated for the Soviet front.

Marshal F. I. Golikov, chief of intelligence for the Soviet general staff, stated that "all reports bearing on German plans were forwarded to Stalin and that they clearly indicated that an attack was being prepared."[3] It was obvious to Golikov, however, that Stalin did not believe a German invasion was an immediate threat. In keeping with the Soviet dictator's conviction, Golikov informed his agents that "all documents claiming war is imminent must be regarded as forgeries from British or even German sources."[4]

Actually, Stalin considered war with Nazi Germany inevitable. However, he was convinced that "it would not occur until 1942 or 1943, leaving him two to three years longer to prepare for it."[5] Meanwhile, for reasons that are unclear, his policy was to lull the Soviet people into a false sense of security.

An example of this was Stalin's reaction to information that German troops were massing on the Soviet border. The British had broken the German secret code, deciphered messages confirming this, and notified Stalin on June 10, 1941, twelve days before the invasion. They supplied accurate data on placement and numbers of German troops, including the names of their commanders and their schedules for moving into action. Three days later, on June 13, the Soviet news agency Tass broadcast a statement believed to have been written personally by Stalin. It warned of "a clumsy propaganda maneuver of the forces arrayed against the Soviet Union and Germany which are interested in a spread and intensification of the war."[6]

A STUNNED REACTION

It has been said that to persuade people successfully, one must first convince oneself. That may be the explanation for Stalin's reaction when the invasion began. He was, by all accounts, completely stunned.

He was awakened at three-thirty in the morning by a phone call from Marshal Georgi Zhukov, the Red Army chief of staff, and informed of bombing raids on Sevastopol, Minsk, and Kiev, and of German troops crossing the Soviet border. Stalin's reaction was silence. It lasted so long that Zhukov asked, "Did you understand me?"[7] Again there was silence. Finally Stalin told him to call a meeting of the Politburo, the select panel appointed by the Central Committee of the Communist party to make quick decisions in urgent matters. At the meeting Stalin seemed unable to grasp the situation. He argued that it couldn't be war because there had not been any declaration of war.

When it was determined that Germany had indeed declared war on the USSR, Stalin still seemed unable to accept it. He authorized Soviet troops to fight back if attacked, but forbade them to pursue any German units that might retreat back across the border. He issued orders that Japan should be asked to mediate between the USSR and Germany with the aim of restoring peace. There was no doubt that he was deeply shaken by the situation, and was not immediately capable of making military decisions.

THE PRICE OF PURGES

The question of Stalin's mental competency at this time remains unanswered. His responsibility for millions of deaths through the famine and purges of the 1930s suggests that he was not merely inhumane, but unbalanced as well. He was paranoid. There could be no doubt of that. It was always those closest to him whom he proved most likely to distrust and have executed. He had strayed far from the principles of communism, and now communism was Stalinism, defined solely by him as an instrument of self-serving illogic and erratic punishment in the interest of maintaining absolute one-man power.

There may also have been an element of self-doubt and guilt in Stalin's immobility when confronted with the sudden invasion. In 1937, on his orders, the command structure of the Soviet military had been purged. Nine members of the Red Army High Command, 3 Soviet marshals, 13 regimental army commanders, 50 corps commanders, 154 divisional commanders, and 8 admirals of the Soviet navy had been convicted of treason on the sketchiest of evidence, and executed. At Stalin's behest, almost 38,000 army officers and 3,000 naval officers had been dismissed from the service.

Faced with invasion, Stalin's reaction may have been caused by his realization that three quarters of the officers commanding his armed forces "had been in active service for less than one year."[8] Years of training were required to successfully command forces in the field. The reconstruction of the Soviet military after the purge was a slow and gradual process. The armed forces of the USSR were not ready to stave off a full-scale German invasion, and the man most responsible for that was Stalin himself.

A NEW COMMAND STRUCTURE

Because of Stalin's policy of denying that the Germans were planning to invade, and because of his belief that while such an invasion was inevitable, it would occur only years in the future, Soviet border troops were caught

Ukrainian civilians watch as German bombing raids begin along the USSR's eastern border in 1941.

completely off guard. At the same time, on the first day of the invasion, devastating attacks by German warplanes destroyed 1,200 aircraft of the Soviet air force. Within seven days the Germans were bragging that "the Führer's offensive has smashed the Red Army to splinters."[9]

There was truth to the bragging, and the situation rapidly became worse in the early days of the war. By mid-July, the German army had taken 480,000 Soviet prisoners and virtually destroyed their tank and armored divisions. The Germans advanced 440 miles in twenty-three days. They were only 200 miles from the Soviet capital city of Moscow.

Stalin pulled himself together. He created the State Defense Committee (GKO in Russian), consisting of the five members of the Politburo with himself as chairman. The GKO would direct all aspects of the war effort. He also established Stavka, the general headquarters of the Soviet supreme command, to see that the decisions of the GKO were carried out. The army general staff was to operate under Stavka's supervision.

Despite the new command structure, it was understood that it was Stalin who was in charge. He would run the war for the Soviets, just as Hitler would often overrule his generals and run the war for the Nazis. The eventual German defeat would reveal Hitler's military decisions to be those of a sadist and a madman. The eventual Soviet victory would not necessarily contradict that the description fit Stalin as well.

STALIN AS
WARLORD

> **Virtually the whole prewar Soviet army was destroyed by 1942.**
>
> Russian military historian Boris Sokolov.

The surprise attack on the USSR was designated Operation Barbarossa by the German High Command. It involved three forces known respectively as Army Group North, Army Group Center, and Army Group South. Spearheaded by a mechanized force of tanks and armored cars, Army Group North's objective was to capture Leningrad. Army Group Center had captured the key city of Minsk and was driving toward Moscow. Army Group South, despite having met fierce resistance in the Ukraine, had overcome it and gone on to overrun the Crimea. This put it in control of farmlands that fed a large percentage of the USSR population, as well as of the Crimea's factories and oil refineries. By the beginning of December 1941, the German front line stretched from the outskirts of Leningrad in the north to the Black Sea port of Odessa in the south, and German forces were on the march well beyond those front lines.

BLIND OBEDIENCE

During the Ukraine campaign, in the September 26 battle for Kiev, the capital city of that Soviet republic, Army Group South had faced massive Soviet forces under the command of Marshal Semyon Budenny. A former officer in the tsarist army, Budenny was derided as a man "with an immense mustache, but a very small brain." Nevertheless, he was a favorite of Stalin's, and his high command was the result of that favoritism. At Kiev his army was exposed to attack from two sides—a pincer movement, as it is known. Most commanders would have withdrawn rapidly and regrouped. Budenny, however, had been ordered by Stalin not to withdraw. The result was a defeat in which the Germans took more than 600,000 Soviet prisoners. Hitler literally jumped for joy, calling the victory the "greatest battle in the history of the world."[1]

The following day Army Group Center, advancing toward Moscow, encircled a major Soviet army and captured another 600,000 prisoners. When he heard the news, Hitler proclaimed that the Soviets would "never rise again."[2] At the time, it seemed like a reasonable prediction. Between June 22 and the end of 1941, Soviet battle casualties totaled 730,000 compared with losses of 250,000 invaders. During that time, the Germans took some four million Soviet soldiers prisoner. In any given battle, the Soviets had outnumbered the Germans. Why then were they so decisively defeated?

The answer is the orders they followed, the tactics and strategy behind the orders, the command structure responsible for formulating those tactics and that strategy, and, ultimately, the one man who insisted that he himself make the military decisions: Joseph Stalin. Time after time Stalin overruled his commanders in the field, the GKO, and Stavka. According to Walter Laqueur, director of the London Institute of Contemporary History, "during the first eighteen months of the war Stalin conducted the war more or less single-handedly."[3] He adds that Stalin's orders were followed because "blind obedience prevailed over common sense; an order had to be carried out however senseless or even suicidal."[4] Russian military historian Boris Sokolov agrees, pointing out that "fear of authority was stronger than fear of death; there was a chance to survive an attack but none to be acquitted by a military tribunal."

Former Soviet commander Konstantin Simonov recalls that "to say aloud that Stalin was wrong, that he commits mistakes, could mean that even before leaving the building you find yourself going to have coffee with Beria."[5] The meaning was clear. Lavrenti Pavlovich Beria was Stalin's ferocious chief of secret police. To take coffee with Beria was understood as a death sentence.

A SPY IS BORN

Lavrenti Beria, like Stalin, was born into a poor family in the tsarist region of Georgia. Twenty years younger than Stalin, he left home at the age of fifteen to work in the oil fields of Baku. Here he became drawn into radical politics, participating in heated discussions about the proper interpretations of the theories of Communist philosopher Karl Marx.

In the summer of 1917, Beria enlisted in the army and fought on the Romanian front. At that time the army was under orders from the Provisional Government, which ruled Russia following the tsar's abdication. When the Provisional Government was overthrown by the Bolsheviks, eighteen-year-old Beria volunteered to return to Georgia as a Bolshevik spy. Georgia was under the control of the Menshevik party, which opposed the Bolsheviks, and when Beria's spying was discovered, he was arrested, imprisoned, and eventually thrown out of Georgia.

Soon afterward, Beria joined the Cheka, the first Soviet secret police agency charged with "combating counterrevolution and sabotage."[6] In 1922 he was named head of the Cheka in Georgia. His brutal tactics in crushing Georgian nationalist opposition to Bolshevik rule earned him a reputation for both Bolshevik loyalty and ruthlessness. These qualities soon brought him to the attention of Joseph Stalin, then the general secretary of the Central Committee of the Communist party.

Stalin was doubtless more impressed by Beria's harshness and accomplishments than by his appearance. Beria was a balding, thin-faced man with small eyes that peered unblinkingly from behind pince-nez glasses. He wore conservative business suits and a gray hat. He looked "more like a teacher or office worker" than the sadistic torturer and murderer that he was.[7]

BERIA'S GULAG

In November 1931, Stalin, now supreme dictator of the USSR, promoted Beria to chief of the Georgian Communist party. This made Beria a public

Lavrenti Beria

figure, no longer operating behind the scenes, and he used his new powers to glorify Stalin. He transformed Stalin's village birthplace into a monument to the leader. He wrote glowing accounts of Stalin's feats as a young revolutionary. When the Stalinist purges of the 1930s began, Beria enforced them in Georgia without mercy.

His reward came in 1938. Stalin appointed Beria deputy to Nikolai Yezhov, head of the NKVD, as the Soviet secret police were now known. Yezhov had succeeded Genrich Yagoda, the NKVD head who had been executed in the purges. Now Stalin feared that Yezhov's role in purging the NKVD of Yagoda loyalists had given him too much power. He had Yezhov arrested and jailed. Following his imprisonment, Yezhov vanished, and Beria became the new head of the NKVD.

Beria's initial accomplishment as NKVD chief was to reorganize the gulag system, the vast network of forced labor camps populated by political prisoners and criminals. He set up a system by which these camps reached and maintained maximum productivity. Under Beria, prisoners worked fourteen- to sixteen-hour days chopping trees for lumber, digging coal and iron ore in deep mines, and performing rote tasks in cotton mills and factories. Production goals were set and met, then increased and met. Early death was a fact of life among the prisoners, but there was a never-ending supply of new slave laborers to replace those who died. By the time the war began, the gulags had long been a key part of the Soviet economy.

THE KATYN FOREST MASSACRE

Beria joined the Communist party Central Committee in 1938. In 1939 he became a nonvoting member of the Politburo. Still head of the NKVD, he personally selected the people to serve in Stalin's household. Like Stalin and Beria, they were all from Georgia. They were all handpicked by Beria and owed their positions to him.

During this period, Stalin trusted Beria with the most delicate assignments. He depended not only on Beria's loyalty and discretion but also on his brutality and lack of squeamishness as well. Beria was perhaps the one man Stalin could rely on to carry out a mass murder of unarmed prisoners of war.

During the period of the nonaggression pact between Germany and the USSR, when the Soviet Union had invaded Poland, some 15,000 Polish officers were among the soldiers taken prisoner by the Red Army. They were sent to three separate prisoner-of-war camps in the Soviet Union. At some point after May 1940, they were sent to a camp in the Katyn Forest on the banks of the Dnieper River near the city of Smolensk. Here their hands were tied behind their backs, and each of the Polish officers was killed with a bullet to the back of the head. The Poles were executed by NKVD security police under the command of Lavrenti Beria. The massacre was ordered by Joseph Stalin.

PUNISHING POWS

There was no valid military reason for Stalin to have ordered the massacre. It was against international law. It was against the common morality practiced by civilized nations. It was one more example of the orders he issued as supreme military commander during the first eighteen months of the war that defied rational explanation.

Some of these orders seemed to reinforce the German strategy rather than strike back at it. German policy was to not adequately clothe, house, or feed Russian prisoners of war. They were deliberately starved and left outdoors in subzero cold to die. "The more of these prisoners who die, the better it is for us," wrote Nazi Minister for the Occupied Eastern Territories Alfred Rosenberg. He added that already "a large part of them have starved, or died . . . [although] there was food enough in Russia to provide for them."[8]

Of the 4 million Soviet soldiers taken prisoner between June 22 and December 31, 1941, only 1.1 million of them were still alive by early 1942.[9] The ordeal of these men — both those who died and those who survived — had been made immeasurably more horrible by Soviet Order 270 signed by the supreme commander Joseph Stalin on August 16, 1941. Order 270 stated that "every officer and soldier who was taken prisoner of war was to be considered a traitor and enemy of the people; their families were to be subject to repression and at the very least deprived of food rations."[10] So it was that while the Germans were starving to death the Soviet prisoners of war, Stalin was punishing the prisoners' families.

THE EVACUATION OF MOSCOW

If the orders issued by Stalin as warlord were incomprehensible, so too were the decisions of his opponent, Adolf Hitler. Like Stalin, Hitler dictated strategy to his generals rather than relying on their expertise. It was his decision to divert armored divisions and tanks from Army Group Center to the battle for Leningrad that slowed down the drive to take Moscow before winter. Many military historians believe that "Germany may have lost the campaign and the war because of Hitler's refusal to allow an immediate drive on Moscow."[11]

It gave the Soviets time to take apart Moscow's industry and relocate it to safer areas. More than fifteen hundred factories were dismantled and moved hundreds of miles east of Moscow to be reassembled and resume production of war materials. Some of these plants were moved as far as the Ural Mountains, western Siberia, and Central Asia. This put a tremendous strain on the railway system, and so the workforce needed to run the factories had to find other ways to reach their new locations. With cars and other motorized transportation scarce, and the roads later washed away by late autumn storms, many of these workers had to travel the long distances on foot. World War II historian Michael J. Lyons reports that "millions of workers had to make the long trek to the east, where they labored as many as fifteen hours a day and experienced deplorable living conditions."[12]

In late September 1941, Hitler evidently had a change of mind and ordered an all-out effort to capture Moscow. German Army Group Center resumed its drive and by early October was within forty miles of the city. By mid-October, they were at the gates to the capital city of the Soviet Union. In a matter of days, observers predicted, Moscow would fall.

CHAPTER
THREE

THE SIEGE OF
LENINGRAD

The children of Leningrad, a city of heavy snows and thick ice, had
always belly-whopped on their sleds through the long winters. The sleds
were toy vehicles of all sizes, in a variety of bright colors. The whir of the
sleds' runners had always mingled with the shouts and laughter of the children at play. But that laughter was silenced in the winter of 1941–1942, and
the sleds were used for other purposes than play. Only the squeal of the
sleds' runners could be heard, and throughout that long winter the nerve-
jangling sound seemed never to stop.

It was the coldest Leningrad winter on record. The average December
temperature was nine degrees above zero Fahrenheit. In January the average temperature was four degrees below zero. In addition to cutting off
food supplies, the German siege had deprived the city of fuel for heating,
and for transportation as well. The trolley lines were shut down and there
was no gasoline for buses or automobiles. Aside from people on foot, only
the sleds were moving along the frozen pavements of Leningrad's narrow
streets and wide boulevards.

The sleds carried a variety of loads. Furniture—a bureau, a table, a
wooden bed—was pulled through the snow from homes that had been

emptied by flight, or by death, to homes where items would be chopped up for kindling to provide heat for those who were left. Frantic parents, gasping in the icy air, towed sick children to overcrowded, understaffed hospitals. Neighbors pulled recently widowed mothers-to-be in the final stages of pregnancy to those same hospitals. The sick, the mentally ill, and the dying were all sled-borne.

Mostly the sleds carried dead bodies. Some were wrapped in sheets, some in hastily hammered together unpainted wooden coffins, and some simply in plain sight, limbs stiff, and eyes too often staring. But there was no place left to bury these corpses. The cemeteries were full. The Leningrad death rate was "rising to 4,000 to 5,000 a day. . . . The dead were left in frozen piles at collecting centers, to be buried in mass graves" at some undefined later date.[1] A few of the exposed bodies were cannibalized by starving people.

ASSESSING THE SITUATION

The siege had been going on since the beginning of September. At that time the German army had been poised to take the city. On September 4 the first German artillery shells fell on central Leningrad. By September 8 the city was encircled by the German army. That was the day Stalin sent General Zhukov from Moscow to Leningrad to assess the crisis.

Zhukov's plane had to wait to take off until heavy cloud cover was available. German bombers were dropping their loads on Leningrad regularly, and the squadrons of fighter planes protecting them were a threat to any Soviet aircraft. As Zhukov's aircraft approached the city, the cloud cover dissipated and the skies became clear. German fighters gave chase, but they did not press an attack. The Soviet plane landed without being fired upon.

The general went directly to the Smolny Institute, where the military commanders of the city were meeting. They were headed by Marshal Kliment Voroshilov. According to Modern History Professor Richard Overy of King's College in London, Voroshilov "was regarded by everyone as a military incompetent, even by Stalin, but he was sent [to Leningrad] as an old Communist to instill the political will to fight on."[2]

A woman pulling a corpse barely draws a glance from passersby along Nevski Prospect, Leningrad's main avenue, during the siege of 1942. Many Russians starved to death during that long winter.

Zhukov listened to Voroshilov and the others describe the military situation, said nothing, and flew back to Moscow. He reported to Stalin that those in command of the city were in a state of panic, that none of the defensive lines outside the city had held, and that little could be expected of the new inner lines of defense dug by the civilians of Leningrad.

Stalin ordered that Voroshilov be relieved of his command. Zhukov was to return to Leningrad immediately to replace him. He left with orders from Stalin "to defend Leningrad to the last breath."

THE EFFECTIVE MARTINET

Georgi Konstantinovich Zhukov "was by any measure a soldier of genius." The unpredictable Stalin could be furious with him, but he nevertheless depended on him. It has been said that without Zhukov, Stalin "might well have lost the war," and that "no one played a greater part in Soviet victory."[3]

The son of a shoemaker, Zhukov was born in a small village outside Moscow in 1896. At the age of nineteen, he was drafted into the tsar's imperial army. After the revolution, he switched over to the Red Army and fought against the counterrevolutionary Whites in the civil war. In 1919 he fought under the command of a military committee headed by Stalin. He became a cavalry officer and then moved on to serve with mechanized forces. During the 1930s, he served as a Soviet military adviser with Communist forces in both Spain and China. At the end of the decade he commanded Soviet forces in a border war with Japan.

Zhukov survived the mass military purges of the 1930s, possibly because of Stalin's high opinion of him. Zhukov was a dedicated Communist, and he was loyal to Stalin. He was one of the very few military men whose opinions could sway the Soviet dictator. Like Stalin, humane considerations were not part of his command style. The lives of the men he commanded were always expendable. It was the winning of the battle, the defeat of the enemy, and the taking of the objective that counted.

Tough and decisive, Zhukov was not a popular commander, but he was effective. Coarse and rough spoken, his sarcastic insults to fellow officers were always laced with profanity. He bullied subordinates and threatened fellow generals who challenged his judgment with court martial and even execution. He used his influence with Stalin to get rid of such colleagues.

In January 1941, Stalin appointed Zhukov chief of the Red Army General Staff. This put him, at the age of forty-three, in a position of authority over experienced generals many years older than he. However, in July, when he argued with Stalin about military strategy, Zhukov was sacked. Angry at having his judgment challenged, Stalin assigned Zhukov to command the Soviet forces defending Smolensk against German Army Group Center. Here Zhukov scored the only major Soviet victory of the early months of the war. It was this feat that may have prompted Stalin to send him to supervise the defense of Leningrad in September 1941.

THE TACTICS OF RESISTANCE

When Zhukov arrived back at headquarters in the Smolny Institute in Leningrad, he threw the maps assembled by the military commanders on the floor, cursed a blue streak, and demanded the facts and figures that would determine his tactics in defending Leningrad. He learned that 636,000 citizens of Leningrad had been evacuated from the city and that these included 216,000 children who had left by early August. He also learned that the German encirclement of the city had prevented the evacuation of another half million women and children.

More than 200,000 Leningrad citizens had enlisted in the army within one week after war was declared. Many more enlistments followed. The majority of these, however, had been marched off to the ever-shifting front to fight in other battles, and were no longer available to defend Leningrad. A citizens' militia had been organized among those who remained. Some 36,000 volunteers—some women, some adolescents, some older men—were being trained to defend the city. They were armed with 22,000 guns of various kinds, which had been supplied by the people of Leningrad. Antitank ditches had been dug and barricades constructed stretching over some seventeen miles of city avenues. Other makeshift barricades dotted many streets. Individual buildings were ringed by sandbags to shield snipers who might fire from behind them. Streetcars and buses had been filled with sand and tipped over to provide cover against any invaders. Slit trenches and air-raid shelters were everywhere.

Georgi Zhukov, who commanded
many of the crucial battles against
German forces

Zhukov incorporated all this into his strategy and built upon it. He positioned antiaircraft guns to be used as antitank weapons. He mined the approaches to the city and created a deep zone of defense in the Leningrad suburbs. He commandeered guns from the Baltic Fleet and used them as cannons. He scheduled a constant artillery barrage to hold the Germans in their trenches. He enlisted the NKVD to crack down on slackers, deserters, and looters. These offenders were shot on sight.

The German troops fought their way through Leningrad's outer defenses. Zhukov positioned snipers and planted booby traps. These resulted in heavy casualties for enemy forces as they advanced. The Germans retaliated. On September 19, German artillery shelled the center city for eighteen hours straight. Luftwaffe (German air force) bombers struck at food storage warehouses, railroad yards, and power plants. Electricity and phone service was destroyed. Fighter planes swooped down on the streets to strafe fleeing civilians.

In the face of this onslaught, Zhukov's tactics managed to hold back the invaders. However, when the suburbs fell and the battle was joined at the last line of defense along the Neva River, Zhukov had forty tons of high explosives distributed among bridges and factories and strategic military positions. If Leningrad fell, its conquerors would not capture its assets. Meanwhile, the resistance held. The Germans had to fight for every yard they advanced.

FACING STARVATION

It was at this point, on September 20, that Hitler changed his mind about taking Leningrad by force. The cost in lives and material was too heavy. He decided on a strategy of siege backed up by ongoing bombing and artillery bombardment. Waterworks, reservoirs, and power plants were prime targets. The German troops encircling the city were ordered to dig in and wait. Hitler believed that lack of food, water, and power would soon force the city into submission.

By the beginning of October 1941, it became obvious to the Soviets that the Germans were not preparing to mount another attack, but were digging in for a siege. Zhukov was recalled to Moscow by Stalin. Here he was assigned the task of defending the Soviet capital against what were thought to be impossible odds. Behind him in Leningrad he left a "population of 3.3 million" with "sufficient food for only twenty days."[4] German warships blocked the port, and German troops had closed off the rail lines and the roads. At this time, the only way food could be brought into the city was via Lake Ladoga. Its southern shore was still held by Soviet troops, but the rail line to transport food from there to Leningrad was held by the Germans. Also, ships were not available at this time to deliver food across the lake.

As the November freeze set in, food was rationed. Workers and soldiers were issued eight ounces of bread daily. Everyone else got four ounces. Ration cards were stolen and forged and sold. Bread was snatched from the hands of those too weak to protect themselves. Pets were killed and eaten. However, there was sacrifice as well. Parents gave their rations to their children. The sick and the old resigned themselves to death and gave their bread to others more fit to survive.

It wasn't enough. Leningrad was starving to death. Only a miracle could save the city from the invaders. But miracles do happen. This one was called "The Ice Road," or "the Road of Life."[5]

"THE ICE ROAD"

By mid-November, Lake Ladoga was frozen over. The Leningrad Military Committee was led by fishermen across the ice to determine if sleds could carry food to the village of Osinovets on the western shore, the first lap of the only possible delivery to Leningrad. The ice would have to be eight inches thick to support the loaded horse-drawn sleds. The inspection determined that in places it was only four inches thick. On November 18, a strong north wind brought a cold front to Lake Ladoga. The temperature dropped; the ice thickened.

The first horse-drawn sleds set out on November 20. The freezing cold and strong winds were too much for the animals. When they collapsed, they were killed and butchered as food for future shipment to Leningrad. On November 22, motorized trucks loaded with food set out across the ice. However, the ice was still too thin in spots to support their weight. Some of the trucks fell through the ice; their drivers drowned. Most, however, made it to Osinovets. Their cargoes added up to thirty-three tons of supplies—a pitifully small amount compared with what was needed.

Osinovets was only the first stop for the caravan. The trucks still had to cross eighteen miles of ice to the village of Kabona. From Kabona the food and other supplies would have to be transported behind the enemy lines at Tikhvin, where the Germans controlled the main railroad between Lake Ladoga and Leningrad. This would involve moving heavy loads through swamps and forests to the loading stations of railway lines still controlled by the Russians. It was decided to build a road for the trucks, first over the frozen lake, and then through the snow-covered wilderness. Because it had to go around the Germans, the road would have to be 237 miles long.

The Red Army was in charge of building the road. Forced labor from Beria's gulag camps worked around the clock in subzero temperatures to complete the road in a little more than two weeks. At first, however, the effort was only partly successful. The thickness of the ice was still unreliable. Trucks could carry only half loads across the ice road. On land, uneven surfaces, drifting snow covering slippery ice, and blinding sleet caused accidents and breakdowns. In early December an average of 361 tons of food and other supplies reached Leningrad every day. This was only a small fraction of what was needed to feed the more than three million people of Leningrad. Food rations were cut, and cut again.

At this time, however, the Soviets attacked the Germans at Tikhvin and recaptured the main Lake Ladoga–Leningrad railroad. During their retreat, the Germans blew up some of the railroad's bridges and sections of track. It was January 1942 before the line was fully operable. However, by then six truck routes had been built across Lake Ladoga. The ice was three feet thick. Caravans of trucks followed one another back and forth across the lake. They supplied Leningrad with fifteen hundred tons of food a day, and then two thousand tons a day. Bread rations were increased in January, and then again in February.

It was also possible now for people to leave Leningrad. By the end of February more than half a million had fled the city to travel the Road of Life across the lake to safety. By April the ice had melted and a fleet of cargo ships had been assembled to transport the food needed by the city, which was still under siege. That siege was still a long way from being over, but for the time being the high-pitched squeals of the tragedy-burdened children's sleds of Leningrad were silenced.

"OPERATION TYPHOON"
THE BATTLE OF
MOSCOW

On October 6, 1941, Stalin recalled General Zhukov from Leningrad to Moscow. Zhukov arrived at dusk the next day and went straight to the private living quarters of the Kremlin, the capitol building of the Soviet government, to see Stalin. He found the Soviet dictator in bed, suffering from a severe attack of influenza. With a trembling hand, Stalin pointed to a map showing German advances in the area immediately west of Moscow. "Look, we're in serious trouble," he told Zhukov. He then ordered him to leave at once for the front and report back to him by telephone at any hour of the day or night. "I'll be waiting for your call," he said, stressing the urgency of the situation.[1]

THE VULNERABLE CITY

Although the Germans had cut many of the telephone lines, Zhukov managed to reach Stalin at two-thirty on the morning of October 8. His report was discouraging. The enemy had broken through at many points along the front. There was actually no continuous line of defense between Moscow and the Germans. No Soviet reserve troops were available to close the gaps in the line. The enemy outnumbered Soviet forces in manpower, tanks, guns, artillery, and aircraft, and had paused to regroup before mounting a final assault. "The principal danger now is that the road to Moscow is now almost entirely unprotected," Zhukov told Stalin.[2]

Later that day, General Alfred Jodl, chief of Hitler's military operations staff, declared that "we have finally and without any exaggeration won the war!"[3] The Battle of Moscow, designated Operation Typhoon by the Germans, was a success. Jodl took it for granted that Moscow would fall in the next day or two. Many people in the Soviet capital city itself also thought Moscow was doomed.

Zhukov had little reason to think otherwise. By this time, in the Soviet Union, "Hitler was master of an area twice the size of France."[4] It was not in Zhukov's nature, however, to dwell on defeat. Instead, he focused on the situation at hand, the deployment of the forces available to him, and devising a plan to defend the supposedly indefensible city.

The army at Zhukov's disposal consisted of 90,000 troops, reduced by capture and casualties from the 800,000 soldiers who had filled its ranks in September. It would have to fight along a 150-mile front under attack by a German army, which, before the battle was over, would number more than a million men. Zhukov's immediate problem was the rapid enemy advance toward Moscow. He had to have additional forces to mount an adequate defense. "I must ask you to start shifting large reserves," he told Stalin.[5]

Zhukov was in luck. At this time, Stalin was receiving reports from Soviet intelligence operatives in Tokyo that Japan had no intention of joining Germany in the war against the USSR, but was stationing its forces to follow up a planned surprise naval and air attack on the United States. Acting on this information, Stalin began to arrange the movement of approximately 400,000 soldiers of the Red Army from Siberia, where they had been poised to repel a Japanese invasion, to Moscow. Such a mass movement of troops, given the inefficiency and constant breakdowns due to weather of the Siberian railway system, would take time. Meanwhile the German advance toward Moscow continued.

RUMORS AND PANIC

By October 14 a series of battles had the Soviet defense forces retreating. In one such battle a recently arrived Mongolian cavalry division charged the German lines across an open field dusted with an early autumn snow. Two thousand of the horsemen were killed. Not a single German died. Other battles resulted in further German advances. The enemy now controlled the road to Moscow, and the city was seized by panic.

The Soviet government was evacuated from its capital city to Kuibyshev, roughly six hundred miles to the southeast. Officials fled Moscow. Cars filled with frenzied government functionaries and their families caused traffic jams on roads to the east. Government buildings stood empty, doors left unlocked and swinging widely, trash baskets black with the ashes of hastily burned documents.

Rumors swept through the population like wildfire. "It was said that a *coup d'etat* had occurred in the Kremlin," recalls one observer, "that Stalin was under arrest, that the Germans were already in Fili on the edge of the city. . . . Crowds surged from street to street, then back again in sudden waves of panic. Already rioting and looting had begun. Stores and warehouses were being emptied by frenzied mobs. The impression spread that there was no more government; that millions of Muscovites had been abandoned to their fate without food, fuel, or weapons. Order was collapsing."[6]

While Zhukov supervised demolition squads placing dynamite at the city's key bridges and railway junctures, Stalin placed the city under martial law. The NKVD was put in charge of enforcing it. Not only looters and rioters were to be "shot on the spot," but defeatists (those spreading rumors that its rulers had deserted Moscow) as well. On October 19, Stalin went on the radio and announced that "Moscow will be defended to the last."[7]

STUCK IN THE MUD

There followed a series of speeches by the usually antireligious Stalin imploring the citizens of Moscow to fight for "Holy Mother Russia."[8] Despite the chaos, the so-called cult of personality—the complete identification of a people with their leader—was once again effective. Stalin's appeals worked. Order was restored. There was a rebirth of patriotism among the citizens of Moscow.

Hundreds of thousands of Moscow women and children were recruited by Zhukov to build barricades for the city's defense. Three rings of these

Moscow citizens dug trenches to trap enemy tanks as part of the defense of that city.

barricades were built around the perimeter of the city. The civilians also dug ditches and constructed tank traps. Auxiliary defense forces were recruited from among the civilian population. They were ill equipped and received no training, but when the battle came, they fought bravely and suffered heavy losses. Zhukov's makeshift fortifications held up against the Germans. These factors, combined with German supply difficulties, saved Moscow from being overrun in October 1941.

Weather was key. In mid-October, sleet mixed with rain started to fall. The roads leading to Moscow were turned into lakes of mud. The cold nighttime temperatures froze them over. The morning sun thawed them out and left a nightmare swamp through which the motorized divisions of the advancing German army couldn't navigate. Jeeps, armored cars, trucks (including flatbeds used for hauling cannons), and even tanks either bogged down in the mud or slithered off in a variety of unintended directions. The skies were overcast even when it wasn't raining or sleeting, and this kept the German air force from bombing Moscow or strafing Soviet troops.

At the end of October the German forces came to a temporary halt, dug in, and waited for reinforcements and replacements to reach them. During the pause, the Soviet reinforcements from Siberia reached the Moscow area. Zhukov held them in reserve. He patched together a force of 240,000 men from survivors of defeated units, Moscow militia, noncombatants (clerks, cooks, hospital attendants, and so forth) from army facilities stationed in the rear, and hastily trained men and women from the suburbs of Moscow. He allotted 100,000 soldiers and 300 tanks from the Siberian units to bolster the western front. This was the last line of defense between the city proper and the German army.

AN ORDER FROM ON HIGH

While Zhukov was making preparations for the mass attack he was expecting, he received an angry telephone call from Stalin. The dictator demanded to know if Zhukov was aware that the Germans had captured Dedovsk, a strategically important town only twenty miles northwest of Moscow. Zhukov admitted that he hadn't heard this. "A commander should know what's going on at the front!" Stalin snapped. He ordered Zhukov to immediately and "personally organize a counter-attack and retake Dedovsk." Zhukov protested that he shouldn't leave his headquarters at the front when a major German attack might begin at any moment. Stalin waved aside Zhukov's objections and commanded him to do as he was told.[9]

When Stalin hung up, Zhukov checked on the status of Dedovsk. He learned that the Germans had not taken it. They had taken a different village, called Dedevo, which was much farther to the west and had no strategic value at all. Nevertheless, Zhukov dared not risk disobeying Stalin. At the head of a small rifle company backed up by two tanks, he retook the unimportant little village from the Germans. He then called Stalin, reported the confusion, and assured him that both Dedovsk and Dedevo were in Soviet hands. Stalin "received the information without comment."[10]

THEY WERE EXPENDABLE

Following the arrival of fresh troops, on November 15 the Germans launched an all-out attack. It was followed up by two more onslaughts on November 24 and November 28. The leading units of the German army were now only twelve miles from the center of Moscow. The Germans, however, were not prepared for the fierceness of the Soviet resistance.

Zhukov had taken Stalin's speech about defending Moscow to the last man quite literally. The general was completely ruthless and expected the men he commanded to follow his orders without question, regardless of how many of their lives might be lost. "If we come to a mine field, our infantry attack exactly as if it were not there," was how he explained his philosophy. "The losses we get from personnel mines we consider only equal to those we would have gotten from machine guns and artillery if the Germans had chosen to defend the area with strong bodies of troops instead of minefields."[11] It was simply not important to Zhukov that ordering soldiers to cross a live minefield was equivalent to throwing their lives away.

Amazingly, the members of the force he had pieced together, many of whom had never seen battle before, believed in Zhukov's methods, believed that he could save Moscow, and obeyed his orders to the letter even when it meant their deaths. Somehow, this cold, hard man commanded their loyalty to an unprecedented degree. He instilled in them what amounted to a fanatic eagerness to die for their country.

An illustration of this is the platoon of Moscow defenders who stopped an attack by twenty and then thirty German tanks with rifles, grenades, and homemade bottled explosives dubbed Molotov cocktails after Vyacheslav Molotov, the Soviet commissioner of foreign affairs. The defenders crippled eighteen of the tanks. At the peak of the battle, a severely wounded political instructor charged with indoctrinating the soldiers in Communist dogma pulled the pins on several hand grenades and threw himself under a German tank. Before doing so, he told the few remaining Soviet survivors of the action that "Russia is big, but there is nowhere to retreat."[12]

COUNTERATTACK AND STALEMATE

Under Zhukov's direction, the defense of Moscow prevailed. December saw Operation Typhoon stopped in its tracks. Heavy snows were falling. Temperatures were dropping to as low as forty degrees below zero. The German attack force had outpaced its supply lines and was short of antifreeze for its armored vehicles. They had to keep small fires going under their tanks to keep the moving parts from freezing. Due to Hitler's optimism that the war would be over before winter, the German soldiers had not been outfitted with cold-weather clothing. Now, efforts to ship such clothing were hampered by snow-covered rail lines with frozen tracks and icy roads that were repeatedly blanketed by snowdrifts. The cold was so bad that butter had to be cut with a saw. To make matters worse, an epidemic of dysentery broke out among the German troops.

Zhukov seized the opportunity to use his fresh Siberian reserves to launch a series of counterattacks. The commanders of German Army Group Central wanted to retreat to a previously prepared line of defense. Orders from Hitler forbade it. He "insisted that the troops must form a number of strong points, called hedgehogs, around advanced supply depots and fight on even if surrounded."[13]

The hedgehog defense was a disaster. It isolated the German positions from one another. During the fierce winter storms, it enabled Zhukov to pick and choose his targets without fear of the Germans being able to reinforce those under attack. His greatest ally continued to be the bitter cold. During the struggle for Moscow, more German soldiers died of frostbite than were killed in battle. The only thing that enabled them to hold out in Hitler's hedgehog defense was an ongoing airlift by the Luftwaffe, which made daily airdrops of food and medical supplies. Army Group Central commanders feared an all-out assault by the Soviets would force their surrender.

Back in Berlin, General Fedor von Bock summed up the situation. "It would be inconceivable," he admitted, "that anyone could reasonably hope to have this operation succeed after our serious losses."[14] This was a far cry from General Jodl's claim only two months earlier that Moscow would fall and Germany would then have won the war.

The decisive Soviet assault the Germans feared never came. Zhukov wanted to deliver what he was sure would be the fatal blow, but he was overruled by Stalin. The supreme commander insisted that the Red Army should spread itself out for an attack on all fronts rather than concentrate on winning the Battle of Moscow. As a result, the series of battles continued indecisively. By March 1942 the Soviet counteroffensive had worn down. The war in general, and the Battle of Moscow in particular, had reached a stalemate. The opportunity to wipe out German Army Group Central had been lost because, once again, Stalin had insisted on dictating the strategy.

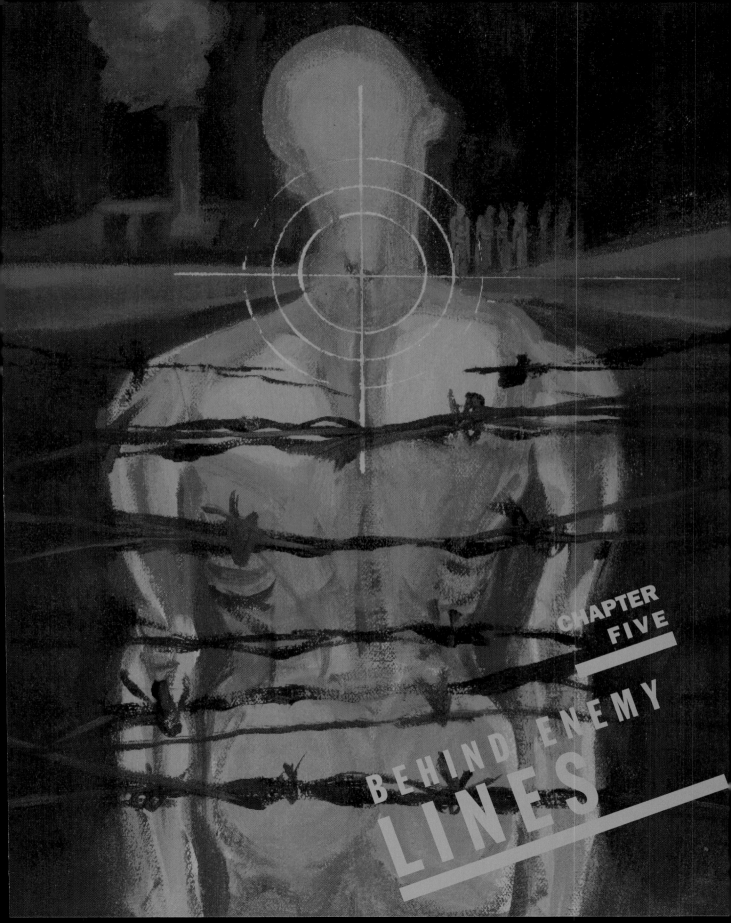

CHAPTER
FIVE

BEHIND ENEMY
LINES

> If you don't want to give away
> All that which you call your country,
> Then kill a German
> Kill a German
> Every time you see one.
>
> Great Fatherland War poem by Konstantin Simonov

After the Battle of Moscow, Red Army soldiers in the front lines stopped taking prisoners. Instead, they killed them. The reason was the atrocities that the Germans had committed. Whenever the Red Army passed through Soviet territory where the Germans had preceded them, they found grim evidence of the enemy's inhumanity. Typical was the fate of a young woman guerrilla fighter named Zoya Kosmodemyanska.

TWO SIDES TO THE STORY

Her story is one of both truth and legend. Zoya was a member of a Communist youth group of underground fighters. They were assigned to destroy anything the advancing German army might find useful. Zoya slipped into a village and was setting fire to some stables when she was caught by the Germans. She was marched down the main street of the village with a sign around her neck identifying her as a saboteur. Then she was tortured and finally hanged. Much later, Red Army troops found her mutilated body dangling from a rope.

Zoya's martyrdom was used for Soviet propaganda in a poem, and then in a play. In the drama, before she dies, Zoya sees a vision of Stalin. He tells her that Moscow still stands, and so she knows that her ordeal has not been in vain. Except for the vision, the story of Zoya is true. There is, however, another side to it.

The young woman may have been captured by the enemy because the local villagers—who did not want their stables burned down—betrayed her. Also, during the purges of the 1930s, both her father and her grandfather were shot and killed by Stalin's henchmen. Her mother had been eager to clear Zoya's father's name, and had encouraged her to join the Communist guerrilla group. Young Zoya had been indoctrinated with the idea of restoring her family's honor by proving her loyalty to Stalin and risking her life for her country.

PARTISANS OR TERRORISTS?

The story of Zoya Kosmodemyanska illustrates the conflicting emotions at work among citizens who have been persecuted by their own government when their nation goes to war. Like those rumored to have betrayed Zoya, some Soviet citizens, particularly in the Ukraine, went over to the enemy. They fought alongside the Germans, participated in the Holocaust in which six million Jews were slaughtered, and volunteered to go to Germany to work in war plants. However, not all volunteered. Half a million Ukrainian women between the ages of eighteen and thirty-five were rounded up and forcibly shipped to Germany to work as domestics or in factories. Under Hitler's orders, four fifths of the forced labor from the Soviet Union came from the Ukraine.

Many Soviet citizens, including Ukrainians, fled to the forests and marshes to form guerrilla forces to harass the German army from the rear. Known as partisans, many of these were Soviet soldiers separated from their units, no longer subject to any specific authority, and trapped behind enemy lines. They were often joined by Communist party members or Jews—two groups known to be killed on sight by the enemy. Usually these partisan groups had to live off the land, which quite often meant stealing from local farms. This sometimes brought them into conflict with farmers who were barely eking out a living from the land. In the autumn and winter of 1941, 30,000 Communist party members sneaked through the German lines, or were parachuted behind them to lead the partisans in actions against the enemy. These actions were ordered by Stalin's State Defense Committee (GKO).

The Nazis reacted brutally to Soviet partisan operations. They regarded the partisans as terrorists, not enemy soldiers, and punished them without regard to international law. An order from Hitler directed German officers to "spread the kind of terror" intended to "make the population lose all interest in insubordination."[1] This resulted in the decision to execute between fifty and one hundred Soviet villagers for every German death caused by partisans. Since the able-bodied men had left most villages to join the armed forces, this meant that thousands of women, children, invalids, and elderly people were shot or hanged by the Germans.

VICTIMS, BULLIES, OR HEROES?

On May 30, 1942, Stalin created the Central Staff for Partisan Warfare. The purpose was to establish absolute centralized control over the various partisan groups. These were organized under Communist party officials or Red Army officers. An NKVD cell was attached to each group in order to make sure that all the members were loyal Stalinist Communists. Negative reports went into Beria's files for later action. In addition, partisan group members who made defeatist statements, or questioned the government's judgment, were considered exceedingly dangerous to morale and immediately executed. Some partisan units were given quotas requiring each member to kill five Germans or five traitors a month, and to take part in at least three raids against the enemy. Failure to meet one's quota could result in punishment by the NKVD.

Much of the Soviet civilian population feared the partisans, and for good reason. When the partisans took actions against the Germans, there were invariably reprisals against townspeople in the area. Survivors might join the partisans out of hatred for the Germans, but others were forced to join the partisan bands by the partisans themselves. Before long, 40 to 60 percent of many partisan bands were made up of those who had been forced to join them.

Nevertheless, the partisans inflicted great damage behind the German lines. They cut telephone and telegraph wires, caused supply train acci-

A crucial element in the disruption of German transportation and fighting was the efforts of guerrilla fighters, like this one who lies in wait with two prepared "Molotov cocktails" for the enemy tanks he knows are coming.

dents by destroying railroad track switches, staged hit-and-run raids on German supply depots, ambushed and massacred German patrols, and committed many other acts of sabotage. German supplies were transported only in vehicles that were heavily armed, and even so they were often subject to sniper fire, hails of bullets, Molotov cocktails, sticks of dynamite, and more powerful bombs.

At blind curves, the partisans would barricade the route while their comrades blocked the road behind a German convoy. Then from hillsides, or the cover of underbrush, the partisans rained death on their trapped enemies. By spring 1943 partisans had destroyed 65,000 German vehicles—including tanks and armored cars—and had blown up 12,000 bridges used by the Germans. This was accomplished in territory the enemy had supposedly conquered and controlled.

After the war Zhukov summed up the contribution of the partisans. "Despite their initial successes up to the Battle of Moscow," he pointed out, "the German forces were confronted with a number of unforeseen circumstances as soon as they invaded the Soviet Union. They never expected that they would have to fight both the Red Army at the front and a powerful guerrilla movement led by underground party units at the rear."[2]

THE RUSSIAN ORTHODOX CHURCH

In the conquered territories, the Germans promoted a rebirth of the Russian Orthodox Church. They hoped it would serve as a rallying point for opponents to the Soviet regime. Hitler, who was as antagonistic to religion as Stalin, thought that at the very least it would make the conquered people easier to manage if they turned to God for relief from the misery inflicted by their conquerors.

Similarly, Communist suppression of religion in the unoccupied Soviet Union was relaxed during the war. This suppression had been in effect since 1922. At that time all assets of the Russian Orthodox Church, to which most Soviet citizens belonged, were seized by the government. Churches and monasteries were closed down. Congregations were disbanded. Many priests were executed. Believers of the Russian Orthodox faith were forced to observe their religion in secret.

Before the revolution, the Russian Orthodox Church had 50,000 priests and 163 bishops distributed over the territory that would become the USSR. By 1941 there were only one hundred priests and seven bishops. They risked their lives to perform religious rites, which under Stalin's communism were against the law. Although it was very dangerous, thousands of practicing Christians received communion in secret masses.

GOOD CHRISTIAN COMMUNISTS

The war changed the status of the Russian Orthodox Church in the unconquered areas of the USSR. Stalin was quick to realize the advantages of bolstering patriotism with religion. He permitted Russian Orthodox churches and seminaries to reopen. The expenses of Church ritual were financed by the government. Stalin even allowed the appointment of a Patriarch of the Church, a national leader who before the war would have been considered a potential rival.

Before the Patriarch was named, a leader of the Church with the title of Metropolitan responded to the invasion by urging the faithful to repel the Germans. During the first two years of the war, the Metropolitan issued twenty-three epistles calling on Christians to fight for Soviet Russia. The Church raised money from congregations to finance a Soviet armored column. Priests and bishops urged the faithful to be true to God and follow Stalin. The cathedrals were crowded with patriotic Stalinist Communists.

The Nazis' attempts to exploit orthodox religion in the conquered territories was nowhere near as successful. Some of the Russian Orthodox bishops the Germans had assumed to be their puppets turned out to have minds of their own. Some were forcibly ejected from their churches; some were executed. One bishop who had urged his flock to pray for a victory against the godless Communists became appalled by Nazi atrocities and withdrew his support from the Germans. The Germans killed him.

UKRAINIAN UNTERMENSCHEN

In the Ukraine, Russian Orthodox Christians were persecuted by the Germans not because of their religion, but because they were considered *untermenschen*—members of an inferior Slavic race. An aim of official German policy was to annihilate the Ukrainians. Hitler's second in command, Reichsmarschall Hermann Göring proposed killing every Ukrainian over the age of fifteen. Even for the Nazi killing machine, however, the extermination of 40 million Ukrainians in the midst of a hard-fought war was not possible.

Nevertheless, thousands of Ukrainians were hanged or shot. Their supposed crimes ranged from not taking off their caps in the presence of a German or slacking off from work, to subversive intellectual activity or suspicion of supporting partisan attacks. Two hundred fifty Ukrainian villages were destroyed, and most of their populations killed, as a lesson to other Ukrainian villages that they must conform to the behavior dictated by the Germans. Thousands more died of a starvation policy deliberately inflicted on them by the Germans.

Food supplies were seized to feed the German army and its hundreds of thousands of horses. So-called superfluous eaters—sick people, old people, Communists, and Jews—were shot. Ukrainian cities were hardest hit. In the city of Kharkov, some 80,000 people died of starvation. Even more died in Kiev as the food rations were cut and medical supplies were withheld. The exact number of Ukrainians who died at the hands of the Germans is not known.

THE SCHUTZMANNSCHAFTEN

Despite the slaughter of Ukrainians, the Germans never tried seriously to exterminate them. The three million Jews of the Ukraine were another matter. Jews were the primary target of Hitler and the Nazis. The policy to wipe them out had started in Germany and had been pursued to a horrendous degree in Poland. The Ukraine was for the Nazis a most promising territory for continuing the genocide of Jews.

There was a long history of persecution of the Jews in the Ukraine. Under the tsars there had been periodic pogroms (anti-Jewish riots) over a period of hundreds of years. At the turn of the twentieth century these had become so common and so deadly that hundreds of thousands of Jews had left the Ukraine, most of them to emigrate to the United States. Later, although communism was supposed to ensure equality for all people, at the local level anti-Semitism (hatred of Jews) remained a fact of life in the Ukraine.

The Germans most certainly knew this. "The Nazis considered the Ukrainians inferior, and the Ukrainians considered the Jews inferior." Of course not all Ukrainians were anti-Semitic. There are many cases of Ukrainians helping Jews or fighting alongside them against the Nazis. However, there was enough Ukrainian anti-Semitism for the Nazis to make use of it. Jew-hating Ukrainians were organized into battalions called Schutzmannschaften. Each battalion had five hundred men. Eighteen and a half such battalions were organized in the first year of the war. They were used primarily to round up and kill Jews, or as concentration camp guards. They would often get drunk before performing mass killings. They "functioned in Poland and other sections of Russia, as well as in the Ukraine itself."[3]

BABI YAR

In late September 1941 a German battalion and a Ukrainian Schutzmannschaften battalion arrived at Babi Yar on the outskirts of Kiev. They rounded up the Jews, 33,000 of them—men, women, children, the sick, and the elderly—and marched them to a ravine on the outskirts of the city. The ravine was a mile long, an antitank ditch that ran between sand dunes. Here the Jews were separated by sex—the males in one group, the women in the other. They were made to take off their clothes. Clothing and valuables were collected. The first contingent of the male group was made to stand on planks at the edge of the ravine. They were shot in the back of the neck and fell into the ditch. Some tried to escape and were shot as they ran. When it came the turn of the women, the executioners made lewd comments as they fired at them.

Over a period of two days, all 33,000 Jews were killed—most of them by Ukrainian Schutzmannschaften. Later, thousands of non-Jewish Soviet prisoners of war and city officials were also executed at Babi Yar. The ditch full of corpses was covered over with quicklime and dirt. Much later the bodies were dug up and cremated.

Babi Yar is the best-known example of a massacre of Jews behind the German lines in the Soviet Union, but it is not the only one. In the Ukrainian city of Dnepropetrovsk, 11,000 elderly Jews and children were machine-gunned. In Kharhovsk, 20,000 Jews were denied food and clothing. Some froze to death. Some died of starvation. The remainder were taken to a gully and shot in small groups. At Odessa 75,000 to 80,000 Soviet Jews were murdered by Romanian troops allied with the Germans.

COSSACKS AND TRAITORS

Traditionally in the Ukraine, the slaughterers of Jews were the Cossacks. These were military tribesmen, fierce fighters with a long and bloody history of service to the tsars. Part of that history was staging pogroms against the Jews as a way of distracting the serfs (those who worked the land) from their exploitation by tsarist landowners. During the civil war that followed the revolution, the Cossacks had fought fiercely on the side of the Whites against the Soviets. Their aim since then had been to establish their own homeland free of Communist domination.

Large numbers of Cossacks welcomed the invasion and offered their services to the Germans. Entire Cossack regiments in the Red Army went over to the enemy. Mostly they were cavalry, superb horsemen who proved invaluable to the Germans in hunting down partisans. They were also used to round up groups of Red Army stragglers who had been separated from their main force. These were dealt with mercilessly.

More than a quarter of a million Cossacks fought with the Germans against the Red Army. However, they constituted only 25 percent of the Soviets who defected to fight against their country. Altogether, an estimated one million soldiers of the USSR went over to the enemy. Their disloyalty was one reaction to the tyranny and oppression of the Stalinist system that had ruled over them.

STALINGRAD!

> **In a race with death, which had no trouble catching up with us and was wrenching its victims out of our ranks in great batches, the army was increasingly pressed into a narrow corner of hell.**
>
> A German officer recalls the horror of Stalingrad.

The Cossack units recruited into the German army became part of the massive offensive mounted against the city of Stalingrad in the summer of 1942. The offensive was partly in response to the outcome of Stalin waving aside Zhukov's strategy in favor of his own during the period after the Battle of Moscow. Stalin belittled Zhukov's military expertise, implying that the general had "the habit of smelling a handful of earth as a means of deciding whether or not to order an attack."[1] Stalin preferred to rely on his own intuition in determining the strategy of the war.

His first mistake was overruling Zhukov's decision to mount a major counterattack against the German army outside Moscow. His second was mounting a series of attacks all along the front. These petered out into skirmishes and accomplished little. Stalin's third mistake was ordering an offensive to retake the city of Kharkov, a vital rail junction, which was key to the German army's supply route. The attack began on May 12, 1942. When it ended ten days later, German forces had captured three Soviet armies. It "was a humiliating failure for Stalin's personal leadership."[2] His humiliation was deepened by defeats in the Crimea and the capture by the Germans of the strategically important seaport of Sevastopol.

"OF THE HAMMER"

One way in which Stalin reacted to such defeats was to blame the Soviet Union's allies—Great Britain and the United States—for not supplying enough aid. He had repeatedly asked both countries to land troops on Soviet soil to fight the Germans, but his requests had been denied. Stalin ignored the fact that the United States had not had time to recover from the surprise Japanese attack on Pearl Harbor in December 1941. He also ignored the effect of the series of defeats the British Army had suffered. Lend Lease—the U.S. program to supply war materials to its allies—was never enough for Stalin. He shrugged off statistics showing that the American merchant seamen sailing the supply ships across the submarine-infested North Atlantic to Murmansk suffered a higher percentage of casualties than any of the U.S. military services.

Stalin's main demand of his allies was that they immediately land troops in France and open a second front in order to force Germany to pull troops out of the Soviet Union to fight the invaders. In May 1942, following the Kharkov defeat, he dispatched Vyacheslav Molotov, the Soviet minister of foreign affairs, to Washington to meet with President Franklin Roosevelt to demand a second front. Molotov had previously negotiated the Nazi-Soviet nonaggression pact in 1939.

When it came to foreign policy, and despite a pronounced stutter, which Stalin somewhat cruelly teased him about, Molotov was Stalin's right-hand man. Born Vyacheslav Mikhaylovich Skryabin in 1890, by the time he was in his teens Molotov was an accomplished violinist. However, he was drawn into the 1905 revolution and changed his name to Molotov, which means "of the hammer."[3] A committed revolutionary, Molotov became involved with Stalin in 1912. He worked closely with Stalin during the Bolshevik Revolution of 1917. In November 1920, Molotov married Paulina Semionova Carpovskaya, a Jewish worker on a sugar-beet farm. Stalin was their best man.

ROOSEVELT AND MOLOTOV

Some years later, during a purge of Soviet Jews, the Politburo, of which Molotov was a member, voted to arrest Paulina. Molotov did not cast a vote either for or against his wife's arrest. She was imprisoned for four years. During that time, "Molotov never brought up the matter with Stalin, with whom he worked on a daily basis."[4]

The relationship between Molotov and Stalin had always been an odd one. At the same time that he entrusted him with important diplomatic missions, Stalin treated Molotov with contempt. Molotov tread a tightrope similar to the one that secret police head Beria walked. The results of being a successful Stalinist were both power and risk.

Yet Molotov proved himself to be a successful diplomat. His Washington meeting with President Roosevelt in May 1942 resulted in a joint Roosevelt-Molotov statement that "full understanding" had been reached "with regard to the urgent task of creating a second front in Europe in 1942."[5] Amazingly, Prime Minister Winston Churchill of Great Britain had not been consulted about this. Nor, of course, was Adolf Hitler aware of such an agreement.

OPERATION BLUE

Hitler's generals wanted to renew their drive to capture Moscow. Hitler rejected this plan. His strategy was to seize the mineral-rich Caucasus mountains in the southern USSR. They were rich in the oil he believed would seal Germany's victory against Great Britain and the United States. Also it would stop the flow of oil to the Soviets and make it impossible for them to continue the war. Code-named Operation Blue, the plan's first objective was to take Rostov on the Don River. However, its primary aim was to cross through the high mountain passes of the Caucasus in order to seize the oil fields on the Caspian Sea.

Preparations for Operation Blue were carried out in secrecy. The British, however, had broken the German secret code and found out about them. They passed the details on to Stalin. He ignored the warnings. Nor did he act on the papers found in a German aircraft, which on June 19 crashed behind Soviet lines. These papers detailed the battle plans for Operation Blue. Stalin thought it was an attempt by German intelligence to mislead the Soviets. He was convinced that the next German attack would be on Moscow, and withdrew troops from other sectors to help defend the city. Zhukov disagreed, but Stalin stuck by his intuition.

On June 28 a massive German force, supported by aircraft and tanks, and flanked by supporting armies of Romanians, Hungarians, and Italians, crashed through the Soviet lines and joined up with German units moving up from the Crimea. The merged force advanced toward Rostov, sweeping aside all resistance. On July 23 as they approached Rostov, the defense forces panicked and fled. The Germans had little trouble occupying the city.

ORDER 227

As news of the fall of Rostov circulated, the panic spread among Soviet forces. Discipline broke down. Whole units abandoned their equipment and ran away. There were mass desertions. In Moscow, civilians whispered that the Red Army was in a state of total collapse.

It wasn't altogether true. Nevertheless, Stalin decided on harsh measures. On July 28 he issued Order 227, which commanded the Red Army to take "not one step further back." It called for the immediate execution of cowards, deserters, and others who panicked in the face of the enemy. Special units were established "in the rear of 'unstable divisions' to shoot to kill in the case of panic and disorderly retreat."[6]

Despite such harsh measures, "Stalin reportedly put out feelers to induce Hitler to make a separate peace." He offered to surrender territory, including part of the Ukraine, in exchange for an end to the war. However, "nothing became of this trial balloon." Meanwhile, the German forces were facing little resistance as they raced toward Stalingrad.[7]

CHURCHILL AND STALIN

Desperate, Stalin notified Prime Minister Churchill: "I must state most emphatically that the Soviet government cannot tolerate the postponement of the second front in Europe until 1943."[8] Churchill replied that he would come to Moscow to discuss the situation face-to-face. Churchill arrived on August 12, 1942. He was preceded by the news that the British had suspended convoys of merchant ships bringing armaments to the USSR. The German submarines were simply too effective. Only eleven of thirty-four ships bound for Archangel had reached their destination. "Why," Stalin asked Churchill sarcastically, "has the British Navy no sense of glory?"[9]

It was an insult, perhaps, that Churchill should have expected. When he arrived in Moscow he had told Stalin that he and Roosevelt agreed that there would be no second front in Europe before 1943. Stalin said that the British and Americans were "going back on their word." Churchill promised a landing in North Africa no later than October, but Stalin was not satisfied. The first day's meeting between the two leaders broke up with bad feelings all around.[10]

The next day Stalin told Churchill that "if the British army had had as much experience of fighting the Germans as the Russian army had, it would not be so frightened of them."[11] Churchill replied angrily. Stalin backed off, complimenting Churchill on his spirited response. However, Churchill's anger did not subside so easily.

Their last meeting was a potluck dinner that lasted half the night. Stalin suggested they invite Molotov to join them because "there is one thing about Molotov—he can drink."[12] After Molotov arrived, the two leaders began to tease him. Molotov had just returned from Washington and Churchill suggested that his return had been delayed by "sneaking off to sample the night life of New York." The stuttering Molotov was alarmed that Stalin might take such a charge seriously. However, Stalin went along with the joke, telling Churchill that Molotov had probably gone "to Chicago, where the other gangsters live."[13]

At two-thirty A.M., after a dinner of suckling pig, the meeting broke up. The issue of a second front was not resolved. Nevertheless, Stalin would later accuse Churchill of going back on his "Moscow promise to open a second front in Western Europe in the spring of 1943."[14]

GENERAL CHUIKOV TAKES OVER

Shortly after Churchill left Moscow, on August 23, the German attack on Stalingrad began with an air raid. Six hundred bombers dropped their loads and "incinerated some 40,000 civilians."[15] When the news reached Moscow, Stalin grudgingly agreed to Zhukov's plan for a counterattack. While Zhukov was assembling his forces, however, the defenders of Stalingrad would have to hold out.

In addition to its strategic importance, Stalingrad had great symbolic value to the Soviets. In the 1918–1921 civil war, the city, then known as

Tsaritsyn, had been a key defensive position blocking the way of the advancing counterrevolutionary forces bent on capturing Moscow. Back then, Stalin had mobilized the defense forces of Tsaritsyn. They successfully repulsed the enemy, and Tsaritsyn was renamed Stalingrad in his honor. Now, in 1942, if Stalingrad should fall, it would be a devastating blow to Soviet morale.

German forces, commanded by General Friedrich Paulus, reached the outskirts of the city on August 24. Soon Germans and Soviets were facing off in the streets of Stalingrad. The Soviet commanding general began to evacuate his troops to the eastern shore of the Volga River. Stalin fired him and replaced him with General Vasily Ivanovich Chuikov. A crude and rugged man with a mouthful of gold teeth, Chuikov rallied the defenders and set up a command center on the Stalingrad side of the river. Here his forces guaranteed the operations of the ferry line, which brought them food and ammunition.

SERGEANT PAVLOV'S HOUSE

Throughout September, the Soviets offered stiff resistance. The enemy paid dearly for every foot of ground taken. During a battle for the Central Railway Station, the terminal changed hands fifteen times. During the day Chuikov's troops retreated house by house, block by block. At night they staged fierce counterattacks and often retook the lost ground. There was no such thing as a clearly defined front line.

Some of the defenders had the advantage of knowing the city, while the Germans had to fight on unfamiliar territory. "Pavlov's house" was a strategically positioned landmark. "A four-storied house . . . it was seized by Sergeant Pavlov of the 13th Guards Division who filled it with sixty men, mortars, heavy machine guns, and antitank weapons. Snipers operating from the third story could pick off any movement on the ground and by mining the square Pavlov held off any tanks. The house came under artillery and mortar fire as well as bombing; but for fifty-eight days Pavlov succeeded in beating off every attack."[16]

Despite such stubborn resistance, the Germans had split Chuikov's forces in half. Troops under his direct command had their backs to the Volga River, holding a patch of ground only a thousand yards from the banks. However, the Germans were exhausted after fifteen days of uninterrupted day- and nighttime fighting. There was a welcome pause in the action.

ZHUKOV'S WINTER OFFENSIVE

By November, German troops had captured most of the Stalingrad factory district. On November 9, Paulus attacked Chuikov's forces with seven divisions. After fierce fighting, the Germans took some ground, but the offensive ground to a halt on November 12. Another stalemate developed.

At midnight on November 18, Chuikov received word that the Germans were about to be cut off by a massive counteroffensive. Zhukov was ready to strike. His force consisted of more than one million men. Chuikov's troops would have to go on defending their position for another six weeks, but the Red Army was on the march.

To concentrate the attack on Stalingrad, Paulus's forces had fallen into a wedge-shaped triangular formation. Stalingrad was the pivotal point. Outside the city the German army was spread out along a two-hundred mile front. Zhukov's forces circled behind them from both north and south, in a carefully planned pincer movement. Early winter was again on Zhukov's side. Hitler had still not outfitted his troops with adequate cold-weather gear. German soldiers fell victim to the freezing cold at the same time the Soviets descended on them.

The two Red armies met and encircled the enemy, cutting off their supply lines. They captured twenty-two divisions. Many of the troops were Romanian, Hungarian, and Italian. As their food and ammunition was used up, they threw down their arms and surrendered. Feeding and housing great numbers of prisoners became an insurmountable problem. Often, the Soviets could not prevent their prisoners from starving to death. In his highly acclaimed account of the Battle of Stalingrad, *Enemy at the Gates*, author William Craig describes an attempt to feed Italian prisoners: "In a camp at Tambov, north of the Don, Italian soldiers crowded around a gate as Russian troops dumped cabbages from a truck onto the snow. Then thirty thousand prisoners rioted and fought each other for the food. Guards shot those they caught in the act of murder."[17]

Although Soviet forces ultimately kept Stalingrad out of Nazi hands, the once thriving city lay in ruins by December 1942.

THE ICEBERG

In Stalingrad, Paulus and his forces were now cut off from what was left of the main body of his army. On November 23, Paulus telegraphed Berlin, reporting "murderous attacks on all fronts. . . . Arrival of sufficient air supplies is not believed possible, even if weather should improve. The ammunition and fuel situation will render the troops defenseless in the very near future. . . . Paulus."[18]

Hitler replied that the "Sixth Army will adopt hedgehog defense. . . . Present Volga front and northern front to be held at all costs. . . . Supplies coming by air."[19]

Paulus knew that the hedgehog defense had cost the Germans heavily in the Battle of Moscow. Nevertheless, and despite the fact that the supplies by air never arrived, he obeyed Hitler's order. It would be treason to disobey. One result of this was that the pressure continued on Chuikov's troops on the banks of the Volga.

Chuikov's situation was desperate. Large chunks of ice floating on the Volga were stopping the ferries from running. The ice was blocking the channel between Zaetseuski Island in mid-river and the shore. Soviet reinforcements on the opposite bank couldn't reach them. Food was running out, and they were short of ammunition. In early December it seemed that there was no way they could withstand another attack by the Germans.

Hope was renewed, however, when a massive iceberg was pushed past Zaetseuski Island by a swift river current backed up by a gale force winter wind. Chuikov described its effect: "Smashing everything in its path, it crushed and pulverized small and large ice floes alike, and broke logs like matchwood." The giant mass of ice settled just opposite Chuikov's bunker. It formed a bridge to the other side of the Volga. Using wooden planks, a road was formed, and a highway for sleighs was built. Chuikov's forces were resupplied and reinforced.[20]

THE END OF THE BATTLE

Now it was Paulus who was trapped. Outside the city his troops had been routed, and he was surrounded by forty-seven divisions of the Red Army.

In early January 1943 the Soviets offered him surrender terms. He refused them. The Germans were then bombarded with the heaviest artillery barrage of the war. On January 17, Paulus again refused to surrender. On January 30, Hitler promoted Paulus to the rank of field marshal.

The next day, January 31, the Red Army learned that Paulus and the last remnant of his fighting forces were holed up in the huge Univermag department store in the center of Stalingrad. The building was shelled and then Soviet soldiers forced their way in with flamethrowers. They found Field Marshal Paulus in a back room, lying on a bed, unshaven and defeated. He was taken prisoner.

Hitler was furious. One hundred and forty-seven thousand German soldiers had died in the Battle of Stalingrad. Ninety-one thousand had been taken prisoner. It was the second of the three turning points in the Nazi invasion of Russia. The Battle of Moscow had been the first. The third would be the Battle of Kursk, "the greatest tank battle ever fought."[21]

CHAPTER
SEVEN

TACTICS, TANKS, AND
LIBRARIANS

> **The blockade is not yet completely broken.
> Farewell, my loved ones. I am going
> To my ordinary, dangerous work
> In the name of the new life of Leningrad.**
>
> Poem written by Olga Berggolts during
> the final year of the Leningrad siege

As the Battle of Stalingrad was drawing to a close, Stalin issued orders for the Red Army to proceed with plans for "War Game No. 5," the code name for the campaign to relieve the siege of Leningrad.[1] Although many people had been evacuated from the city, and food was available if still not plentiful, those who remained were living in deplorable conditions. The water supply had been shut off, there was no electricity, and little fuel. Almost everyone had scurvy (a disease caused by a lack of vitamin C), and a typhus epidemic had been contained with difficulty. The greatest threat to survival was the filth in which people were forced to live and the spread of disease, which such filth encouraged.

THE LENINGRAD LIBRARIANS

The women of Leningrad organized to fight the festering filth. More than 300,000 people participated in a massive citywide cleanup campaign. Among them was a group of librarians.

During the siege, the great Leningrad Public Library never closed. Its services were key to the survival of the city. The librarians "answered a thousand questions put to them by the military and civil authorities: How could Leningrad make matches? How could flint and steel lighters be manufactured? What materials were needed for candles? Was there any way of making yeast, edible wood, artificial vitamins? How do you make soap? The librarians found recipes for candles in old works of the eighteenth century." One hundred thirty-eight Leningrad librarians died during the siege.[2]

One who lived was Hilma Stepanovna, who had been permanently deafened by a German bomb. With her five-year-old son, she had gone with other library workers to help clean up the streets. She and her son were arrested by Beria's NKVD as "enemies of the people."[3] She had been married to a newspaper editor who had been executed in 1940 for writing treasonous articles. Now she and her son were exiled from the city. As late as 1964, she and her son were denied permission to return to Leningrad by the Soviet government. No explanation was ever given for her arrest.

BACK TO THE DRAWING BOARD

In preparation for the implementation of War Game No. 5, a group of Red Army generals and their commander, Marshal Kliment Voroshilov, met with Major L. S. Barshai of the Leningrad Subway Construction Trust on Christmas Day 1942. Major Barshai had come up with a way to deal with the thinness of the ice on the Neva River so that Soviet tanks would be able to cross it. He had devised a wooden frame that was bolted to the tank treads so that the weight of the tank would be distributed over a wider area of ice.

As Leningrad citizens observed a sparse Christmas, the first tank started out across the ice with a group of officers trailing behind on foot. The tank and the group had gone about 150 yards when the ice began to crack in all directions. Quick-thinking officers pulled Marshal Voroshilov back from the gaping hole as the tank plunged into the water and sank. The tank driver escaped and bobbed to the surface where he was handed a flask of vodka. Marshal Voroshilov ordered that he be awarded the Order of the Red Star. He also ordered his subordinates to go back to the drawing board.

Despite such setbacks, the attack on the Germans laying siege to Leningrad began a little more than two weeks later, on January 12, 1943.

Just before eleven P.M. on January 18, the Leningrad government radio station announced that Red Army troops had "broken the blockade of Leningrad."[4] There was dancing in the streets. People hugged one another. There were flags everywhere. It was the 526th day of the blockade and the 637,000 people left in Leningrad could not contain their joy. The siege, they believed, had been broken.

It wasn't so. The blockade had only been partially lifted. The siege would go on for another year. Many more people would die in Leningrad before it was finally over.

OPERATION CITADEL

The partial lifting of the siege at Leningrad coincided with the victory at Stalingrad. The latter was a tremendous boost to the morale of the Soviet people. Stalin's prestige soared. Zhukov was acclaimed as a great military strategist. On the other hand, Stalingrad, with its high death toll, was a terrible blow to the Germans. Their faith in Adolf Hitler was seriously shaken.

Hitler was aware of this as winter turned to spring in 1943. In North Africa, which he had invaded in 1941, his armies were retreating after major defeats by British, American, and French forces. Hungary and Romania, Germany's allies, were putting out peace feelers to the enemy. Berlin was being bombed. Hitler's prestige required a military victory. A target was selected, and a major strike against the Red Army was planned by German Field Marshal Erich von Manstein. It was code-named *Zitadelle* (Citadel). It would go down in history as the Battle of Kursk.

Von Manstein wanted to activate Citadel in April. He believed that a surprise attack would guarantee success. Hitler, however, postponed the operation until July when more tanks would be available. The famous German tank commander General Heinz Guderian opposed Citadel. Germany, he insisted, was "certain to suffer heavy tank casualties, that we would not be able to replace." Told that the attack was necessary for reasons of politics and morale, Guderian asked, "How many people do you think know where Kursk is?"[5]

In fact, there were strategic reasons for targeting Kursk. A city of 120,000 people, it sat on a plateau that overlooked part of a Soviet-held area behind a defensive line roughly 120 miles long and 60 miles wide. This line formed a bulge into the German front, and represented the constant threat of a major Soviet breakthrough. Von Manstein's plan was to encircle the bulge and destroy the Red Army. Tanks would play a major role in this.

ZHUKOV LAYS A TRAP

The Soviets knew that an attack was coming. Stalin believed the Germans would again try to seize Moscow. He wanted to attack the Germans first, before they could strike. He "followed his instinct and called for a preemptive offensive before the German line had solidified."[6]

Zhukov also assumed at first that Moscow was the target. However, he favored a laid-back defense in which the Soviets would simply absorb the initial German attacks and allow them to advance to a point where a large Soviet reserve force could counterattack and wipe them out. When Zhukov received intelligence reports that Kursk, and not Moscow, was the German target, he rejected Stalin's plan for "a preemptive offensive."[7] Stalin now regarded Zhukov as the savior of both Moscow and Stalingrad. He called off the offensive and approved Zhukov's strategy.

Far from the German front lines, in an area around Kursk, Zhukov set his trap. The troops of seven Soviet armies were literally crammed into this territory. The people of Kursk were drafted to help dig trenches in a crisscross pattern, with more trenches backing them up—three thousand miles of trenches in all. Pits with stakes embedded in them were also dug and covered over to form antitank traps. More than 400,000 land mines were buried. Artillery and antitank guns were set up. Altogether, the Soviet forces in front of Kursk included 1,336,000 soldiers, and 3,444 tanks. When the battle was joined, they would face 900,000 Germans backed up by 2,700 tanks.

TAKING THE HIGH GROUND

On July 5, 1943, the Battle of Kursk began with a coordinated barrage by German artillery, Stuka dive-bombers, and the mass movement of tanks. Soviet cannons fired back, and soon infantry units from both sides were

German tanks maneuver through
a cornfield during the Battle of Kursk.

exchanging deadly rounds of small-arms fire. Heavily armored German Tiger tanks crashed through the Soviet defenses, followed by lighter and smaller tanks called Panthers. Soviet shells bounced off the Tigers, but even machine-gun fire proved deadly to the Panthers. "They were easily set ablaze," a German tank officer remembers, "the oil and fuel systems were inadequately protected and the crews were insufficiently trained."[8] One Panther brigade of two hundred tanks stumbled into a Soviet minefield. Thirty-six were disabled. The rest retreated.

Nevertheless, by the end of the day the Germans had broken through the Soviet front lines and advanced eleven miles. An important next objective was a four-hundred-foot-high ridge forty miles south of Kursk. Artillery mounted atop the ridge would cover a vast area between it and the city. German observers could monitor the Soviet forces on the plain below.

The Soviets anticipated the attempt to seize the ridge. The hills around it bristled with rocket launchers, machine-gun nests, and tank traps. Every gully had been turned into a trench filled with infantry. Soviet tanks were ready to do battle with the exposed German tanks moving across the plain.

All day long the battle raged. By nightfall the Germans had advanced six miles, but had still not seized the ridge. They had suffered 25,000 casualties and lost roughly 200 tanks. The battle continued for four more days. On July 8 the Germans broke through the Soviet defenses and blasted their way to the top of the ridge. A savage Soviet counterattack took the ridge back from them. Twice more the Germans seized the ridge, and twice more the fury of the Soviets forced them to give it up. The Germans didn't try again.

HITLER'S INCREDIBLE ORDER

Both sides were exhausted and there was a lull in the fighting. At Soviet First Tank Army Headquarters, Lieutenant General Nikita S. Khrushchev was concerned. "The next two or three days will be terrible," predicted the man who would one day head the government of the USSR. "Either we hold out or the Germans take Kursk."[9]

On July 9 the Germans circled around the Soviet troops to break through an area less strongly defended. Three days later the German command judged their objective to be within their grasp; the Red Army would be destroyed at Kursk. As tanks and men were moving into position, however, an incredible order was received. Hitler had decided to end Operation Citadel. American and British troops had invaded Sicily, and the Italian army had fled from them. Hitler feared that Italy would fall, and that the Balkans would follow. He needed reinforcements and, "since they can't be taken from any other place," he decreed, "they will have to be released from the Kursk front. Therefore, I am forced to stop Citadel."[10]

AN INFERNO OF TANKS

Hitler's order came too late to stop the conflict already in progress. Three thousand German and Soviet tanks faced off in a battle that raged for six days. A German officer described the scene: "Our tanks advanced across the steppe in small groups, using copses and hedges as cover. Initial staccato gunfire soon merged in a great sustained roar. The Russian tanks met the German advance formation flat out. Both sides' tanks were mixed up together, and there was no opportunity, either in time or space, to disengage and reform in battle order, or to fight in battle formation."[11]

Fired at such close range, shells pierced the armor of the tanks and turned them into flaming coffins. Overhead, warplanes of both sides bombed and strafed. Antitank artillery pounded the battle zone. The German tanks had greater firepower, but the Soviets had greater mobility. They dashed in and out among the enemy tanks, inflicting damage and scooting away. A German tank commander described them as "streaming like rats all over the battlefield."[12]

The battle continued in driving rain. Tanks had difficulty maneuvering. Infantry from both sides were mixed in among them. German foot soldiers would run up to the blind spot of a Soviet tank, attach a bomb with sticky tape, and dive for cover. Soviet troops fought them hand to hand. It was fierce and might have gone on longer had not Hitler's order to transfer units from Kursk to Italy been carried out.

According to Zhukov, during the Battle of Kursk "the enemy's losses totaled 500,000 men, 2,000 tanks and self-propelled guns."[13] The Germans were forced to retreat. With Zhukov's massive reserve force in hot pursuit, the retreat quickly turned into a rout.

German resistance continued to crumble through the latter part of 1943. The Red Army struck at numerous points along the enemy's overextended front. Often the fleeing, undermanned German army ran out of gasoline and was forced to leave tanks, trucks, and even jeeps behind. By the end of September, the Soviets had advanced deep into the Ukraine, and controlled large sections of it..

THE LIBERATION OF LENINGRAD

That same month, the Red Army commanders began planning a massive assault to liberate Leningrad. Throughout 1943 the city had suffered from constant bombing and shelling by the Germans. Efforts by the Soviets to dislodge the enemy had involved savage fighting and heavy casualties, but had not succeeded. Now, with the Germans retreating on other fronts, the time seemed ripe to end the siege of Leningrad.

Beginning on November 5 and continuing through the end of the year, enormous amounts of equipment were moved into position for the assault. One and a quarter million Soviet soldiers assembled to attack the 741,000 Germans just outside Leningrad. By early January the Soviets were ready. Lieutenant General Leonid A. Govorov climbed a tall hill to survey the terrain. When he returned, he addressed his officers. "On the tempo of our advance," he warned, "hangs the fate of Leningrad. If we are held up, Leningrad will be subjected to such a terrible shelling that it will be impossible to stand it—so many people will be killed, so many buildings demolished."[14]

On January 14 the assault began. Artillery shells thundered over the heads of the people of Leningrad to fall with devastating accuracy on German trenches. By January 19, the Soviets had stepped up the offensive. A rumor circulated in Leningrad that once the blockade had been lifted, those who had lived through it would be sent to rest homes for two months. By January 17, the Germans were in disorderly retreat from Leningrad. On January 27, 1944, a rainbow of rockets and other fireworks erupted over the Palace Square in Leningrad. After nine hundred days, the siege was finally and completely ended. The following months would mark the start of the Red Army's unstoppable march westward toward Germany.

THE SCORCHED EARTH
POLICY

> **I am tired and sick of war. Its glory is all moonshine. It is only those who have neither fired a shot nor heard the shrieks and groans of the wounded who cry aloud for blood, more vengeance, more desolation. War is hell.**
>
> Union General William Tecumseh Sherman of Civil War fame

In September 1943, Hitler authorized a retreat of German armies in the Soviet Union. At the same time he ordered that the Scorched Earth Policy begin. This was a plan ordering the German military to destroy everything in its path as it withdrew from Soviet territory. Behind them they would leave a desolate terrain with nothing that could be used by the Red Army.

FORGING A WASTELAND

The path of the German retreat included fruitful farmlands, regions rich in coal, and miles of densely wooded forests, which had shielded partisan snipers and which could serve as cover for attacking Soviet troops. There were large herds of cattle, sheep, and horses. There were whole cities with factories and power plants. There were many bridges and miles and miles of railroad tracks. There were thousands of able-bodied men and women whom the Soviets might draft for war work or as soldiers.

Field Marshal von Manstein struck at the Soviet population first. Hundreds, and then thousands, of men and women were herded ahead of the retreating German army. On foot and in peasant carts, they clogged the roads, impeding the mechanized German units. It was more important to keep the Red Army from putting them to use than it was to speed up the retreat of jeeps and trucks and tanks. Besides, if they moved too slowly, they could always be shot and left by the side of the road.

Livestock, a possible source of food for a Soviet army that was advancing so swiftly it was outdistancing its supply lines, was seized by the Germans. They drove half a million cows, sheep, and horses ahead of them. They seized what food they could carry and destroyed what they couldn't. They burned acres and acres of wheat fields and orchards, leaving children and old people behind to face starvation.

THE ZAPOROZHYE DAM

Smolensk, a factory city of 150,000 people, was torched by the retreating Germans and almost completely destroyed. All along the line of retreat bridges and dams were blown up to slow down the Soviets. However, there was one structure that Hitler did not want destroyed: the Zaporozhye Dam on the Dnieper River.

The Zaporozhye Dam, a hydroelectric plant, provided power to the territory in the western Ukraine, which was still controlled by the Germans. That power fueled the factories producing armaments for von Manstein's forces. Hitler regarded the dam as crucial to holding the Soviets at bay. He ordered that it be defended to the last man. However, when the Soviets attacked, they outnumbered the German defenders ten to one. During a doomed holding action, von Manstein ordered the dam seeded with two hundred tons of dynamite. On the night of October 14, 1943, the few German defenders remaining alive were ferried across the river to safety, and the dynamite was detonated. The dam crumbled and the torrent of waters behind it cascaded down the Dnieper River. The Soviets had been denied the power station, but the Germans had lost a priceless war production asset.

THE TEHRAN MEETING

At this time plans were being made for a face-to-face meeting of the leaders of the USSR, the United States, and Great Britain. Prime Minister Churchill and President Roosevelt suggested Cairo in Egypt, Baghdad or Basra in Iraq, or Asmara in Ethiopia as places to meet. Stalin turned them all down. He wanted to meet in Tehran, Iran, insisting that from there he would be able to continue "the day-to-day running of the staff."[1] Finally, Churchill and Roosevelt agreed to meet in Tehran.

Stalin and President Roosevelt had never before met. The president recognized that Soviet troops were steadily driving the invaders from their country, and that soon they would be on the march through Eastern Europe toward Germany. Considering both its victories and its sacrifices, the USSR had earned a significant role in setting the boundaries of post-war Europe. It was important to Roosevelt to establish a working relationship with Stalin.

Sensing the antagonism between Stalin and Churchill, the president exploited it. "I began to tease Churchill about his Britishness," Roosevelt recalled later, "about his cigars, about his habits. It began to register with Stalin. Winston got red and scowled and finally Stalin broke into a deep, hearty guffaw. It was then that I called him Uncle Joe."[2]

It broke the ice. Once Churchill calmed down, the three leaders got to work. Roosevelt and Churchill agreed to Stalin's demands to open a second front in France no later than May 1944. Stalin agreed that after Germany was defeated the Soviet Union would declare war on Japan. Stalin demanded that the Soviet Union be allowed to keep the 76,500 square miles of Poland it had seized under the 1939 pact with Germany. Aware that Russian troops were already about to retake that territory, Roosevelt and Churchill agreed to extend the Soviet Union's border west into Poland and to compensate Poland by ceding it territory in eastern Germany. Stalin got pretty much all that he wanted at Tehran.

PUNISHING THE INNOCENT

The Soviet leader was riding high. As his troops drove the Germans westward and reclaimed lands they had occupied, he authorized Beria and the NKVD to deal with those who had collaborated with the Germans. From the earliest days of the Soviet Union, Stalin had been deeply suspicious of the many non-Russian Soviet states that wanted nations of their own. First the tsars had made them part of Imperial Russia, and then the Bolshevik/Communists had forced them into the Soviet Union. Some, but by no means all, had collaborated with the Germans, welcoming them as liberators.

Joseph Stalin, Franklin Roosevelt, and Winston Churchill meet for the first time in Tehran, Iran, in November 1943.

Now it was payback time for the collaborators. Beria encouraged Stalin to act harshly. Behind the advancing Soviet armies, the NKVD moved in to round up and execute those suspected of pro-German activity. Local officials in liberated villages, fearful of being singled out and blamed for inadequate resistance to the Germans, exaggerated the figures of collaboration to spread the blame over whole populations. Many old scores were settled in the name of punishing collaborators.

Stalin's campaign against alleged traitors was also used to try to stamp out the spirit of nationalism among the various ethnic groups. Entire ethnic populations were exiled from their homelands between October 1943 and June 1944. Among those affected were the Balkars, the Ingushes, the Islamic Karachais, the Meshkhetians of southern Georgia, Soviet Germans, Greeks, and Kurds, Crimean Tartars, Kalmyks, and—most notably—the Chechens.

Chechnya, in the Caucasus, with its population of a little more than a million people, was a particular target of the NKVD. The Chechens were Muslims with their own language and traditions. They had long resented first Russian, then Soviet, rule. They were a fiercely independent people, and unlikely to have welcomed authority by the Germans any more than by the Soviets. Nevertheless, because of their history of rebelliousness, Chechens were particularly chosen by Stalin and Beria for "collective punishment."[3]

How this was carried out is described by Professor Richard Overy in his book *Russia's War: Blood Upon the Snow*:

In February 1944 NKVD troops entered the tiny republic as if on a military exercise.... On the evening of February 22, the annual Red Army Day, the population was assembled in the village squares to celebrate. The crowds were suddenly surrounded by NKVD troops and the deportation order read out to them. Scuffles broke out as unarmed Chechens fought to escape. Some were shot down. The rest were ordered to pack at once, no more than a hundred pounds of baggage per family. Heavy snowfalls and frost hampered the operation, but within twenty-four hours most of the Chechen population was loaded into trucks and trains, destined for Siberia. In one township those left behind were gunned down, buried in pits, and covered with sand.

At Beria's request, Stalin awarded 413 medals to NKVD troops who participated in the campaign against "traitors to the fatherland."[4]

THE D-DAY LANDINGS

Meanwhile, the Red Army was continuing to drive the Germans out of the USSR. As the Soviets advanced they found increasing evidence of Hitler's Scorched Earth Policy. On April 10, 1944, the Red Army liberated the key port of Odessa on the Black Sea. The retreating Nazis had executed 82,000 civilians and transported 78,000 to Germany to work as slave laborers.

On May 9, Sevastopol was liberated. Twenty-seven thousand civilians had been slaughtered by the Germans and 42,000 had been shipped to Germany. Only three thousand civilians remained, and the city was in ruins.

As Red Army victories piled up, Stalin's demands for a second front in Western Europe were finally met. On June 6, D Day, the Western allies landed 175,000 troops on the beaches of Normandy in France. They were preceded by thousands of U.S. paratroopers dropped behind enemy lines whose objective was to join up with French partisan forces and seize bridges, airfields, power plants, and other military objectives. Hundreds of thousands of reinforcements would follow. Now Hitler was suffering massive attacks from both east and west.

Fifteen days after D Day, the Soviets staged massive bombing raids against supply troops in areas to the rear of the German retreat. They used not only conventional bombers but all kinds of aircraft capable of dropping explosives. Some raids were carried out by the 46th Guards Women's Night Light Bomber Regiment, an outfit run entirely by women, which included mechanics, pilots, and other personnel. Some of the women dropped their bombs from biplanes (old-fashioned civilian aircraft with double-wing spreads and open cockpits), flying low, at great risk from anti-aircraft fire, to assure accuracy. Twenty-three of these women were awarded medals as "Heroes of the Soviet Union."[5]

THE SLAUGHTER OF WARSAW

By now some Soviet troops had reached foreign soil. They had crossed the borders of Germany's ally, Romania, and were on the move toward its capital, Bucharest. On July 13 they liberated the Lithuanian capital of Vilnius. On July 20 they pursued the retreating Germans into Poland and were proceeding toward Warsaw.

On August 1, 20,000 poorly armed Poles rose up against the Germans in Warsaw. Snipers fired on German troops from doorways and windows. Homemade bombs were hurled. Crude mines were rigged up and exploded under trucks and tanks. The rebels succeeded in seizing large parts of central Warsaw. The battle went on for two months, but in the end the Poles had neither the manpower nor the arms to hold out against the German army. With the Red Army on the banks of the Vistula and in sight of the city, the Poles were forced to surrender.

What followed has been called "the largest single atrocity of the war."[6] German troops went on a rampage. Hospitals were set afire with doctors, nurses, and patients imprisoned inside. Thousands of women and children were murdered. Those who fled through the sewers were driven above ground by gas and killed. Buildings were destroyed brick by brick, streets torn up stone by stone. Warsaw was completely demolished. Two hundred and twenty-five thousand Polish civilians were murdered.

PRESCRIPTION FOR VENGEANCE

As summer was ending, all the Soviet territories occupied by the Germans had been retaken by the Red Army. The retreating Germans had executed a total of 1.8 million civilians, 1.3 million had been transported to Germany as slave laborers, and 11 million people had been left homeless by the Scorched Earth Policy. Soviet troops could not believe the devastation and human suffering through which they advanced. This was their country, and it had suffered more from the enemy than any other country in recent history.

Revenge was the byword for the Red Army now. The horrors that Soviet soldiers had seen would incite the atrocities that Soviet soldiers would commit. As the poem by W. H. Auden points out:

I and the public know
What all schoolchildren learn,
Those to whom evil is done
Do evil in return.[7]

CHAPTER
NINE

VENGEANCE AND
VICTORY!

> **Well then, imagine a man who has fought from Stalingrad to Belgrade—over thousands of kilometers of his own devastated land, across the dead bodies of his comrades and dearest ones! How can such a man react normally? And what is so awful in his having fun with a woman, after such horrors?**
>
> Stalin excuses rapes of Yugoslav women by Soviet soldiers to Yugoslav Communist leader Milovan Djilas.

As 1944 drew to a close, the citizens of the Soviet Union set about rebuilding their ravaged cities. In Leningrad 15 million square feet of housing had been destroyed by German shells and bombs. More than 716,000 people had been left homeless. Five hundred twenty-six schools, 840 factories, and 300 historical monuments had been destroyed. The Hermitage, founded in 1764 and housing one of the world's greatest art collections, had been hit by thirty-two shells and two bombs.

Leningrad was to the Soviet Union as New York City is to the United States. It was a great and historic city with a symbolism reaching far beyond the bricks and mortar, which had been reduced to rubble. From all over the Soviet Union people rallied to help in what would be known as the Leningrad Renaissance.[1] As workers came to rebuild the city, the population doubled. The streets were cleared, and the slow process of renovation began. Leningrad was putting the war behind it, and there was once again the trill of laughter from little girls skipping rope as brick was piled on brick, and buildings rose to greet the sunlight of a new day.

REBUILDING A NATION

For the civilians of the Soviet Union, it was like waking from a long sleep. There was so much to be done, but there was also the will to do it. "I sometimes wonder where I find the strength," said a sixty-year-old village blacksmith with two sons still at the front. "But since we've been freed, it's like a load dropped from your heart — I work and don't feel the least bit tired."[2]

Former partisans formed village governments, found pipes to restore water supplies, repaired electric generators so that now there was light, and distributed food and clothing. Buried treasures, hidden from the Germans, were dug up. As much as possible, the land was reclaimed. Crops were planted. Stray farm animals were recaptured. Old-fashioned barn dances were held. Schools were reopened for the children.

There were "thousands of wandering children, their parents killed, or deported to slave labor camps."[3] They were gathered up and taken to receiving centers. Some were reunited with their parents. Some were adopted. The majority ended up in group orphan homes on collective farms or in the cities.

In Stalingrad, booby traps were still a problem. The Germans had planted explosives everywhere. Some of the houses had been wired to blow up when the electric power was restored. Nevertheless, the people searched the rubble for anything that could be used to rebuild their city. "In settlements and gorges, dumps and attics," wrote a city official, "little by little, everything was swept up and put to use."[4]

Irina Chervyakova, a seamstress in Sevastopol, organized eighteen fellow workers to rebuild their factory. They went on to help rebuild a railroad station, a community center, and a road. Many other such women worked at tasks that had little to do with their former jobs. Cleaning women toiled as bricklayers. A kindergarten teacher explained why she was doing manual labor to rebuild her city. She told how her two little girls had been killed, adding that she was avenging them by her work. It was a constructive vengeance, very different from that of the Soviet soldiers pursuing the enemy through the countries of Nazi allies.

THE BATTLE OF THE BULGE

The war was not yet over as the end of 1944 approached. As the first Soviet forces reached Prussia in East Germany, the American army had fought its way from the beaches of France to the hilly forests of the Ardennes in

Belgium. On December 16, 1944, American infantry and paratroopers suffered a surprise attack in force by German army troops. The conflict that followed would go down in history as the Battle of the Bulge.

Hitler planned the offensive himself. Not one of his generals thought it would work. Hitler overruled them. He called it "the greatest bluff since Genghis Khan."[5] He predicted that the sudden onslaught "would divide the British and American forces," and that "the British would have to pull another Dunkirk" and once again evacuate their forces from the continent of Europe.[6]

Unfortunately, the supreme commander of the allied forces, Dwight Eisenhower, and his chief aide, General Omar Bradley, agreed with the assessment of the German commanders. The Americans and British were convinced that "it would be unprofitable to the Germans to make such an attack. [It] would be a strategic mistake for the enemy."[7] However, precisely because it was judged so unlikely, Hitler's strategy proved devastating to the American troops trapped in the bitter winter snows of the Ardennes.

Their situation was desperate. They were cut off and surrounded. They were being heavily bombarded by artillery. They were under constant attack by crack German troops, some of them speaking flawless English and wearing American army uniforms The weather was interfering with efforts to drop food and medical supplies by parachute. American and British tanks, and trucks carrying reinforcements, were mired down in the snow and couldn't reach them. It seemed as if Hitler's unsound strategy was going to work.

On January 6, 1945, Stalin received an urgent message from Churchill. There was grave concern that Hitler might withdraw additional forces from the east to push the German assault in Belgium to a successful conclusion. He pleaded for a Red Army offensive to keep German forces pinned down fighting the Soviets.

Stalin replied that Soviet forces would "commence large-scale offensive operations against the Germans along the whole Central Front."[8] The Red Army offensive was launched on January 12. Stalin "was delighted to put the Allies in his debt."[9] It also—and most significantly—made it possible for the Red Army to firm up its occupation of the countries of Eastern and southern Europe, and put it within striking distance of Berlin. Before long, the American army was recovering from the Battle of the Bulge and had crossed the Rhine into Germany.

THE YALTA CONFERENCE

By January 29, Red Army forces under Marshal Zhukov were within sixty-seven miles of Berlin. A blinding blizzard kept them from continuing their drive to seize the city. A week later, on February 6, General Zhukov received a call from Stalin. Zhukov was ordered to halt the drive on Berlin and redirect his drive to Pomerania, a province of Germany north of Berlin. The reasons for Stalin's order have never been explained. It may have been to give his supply lines a chance to catch up with his fighting forces before what would undoubtedly be a bitter battle for Berlin. It may have been because he wanted to capture still more German territory before Berlin fell and an armistice prevented further expansion. Or it may have been that he wanted the Americans and British to suffer more casualties to drive home to them what their postponement of a second front had cost the Soviet Union.

Stalin had made the call from Yalta, a resort city in the Crimea. He had arrived there two days earlier for a second "Big Three" meeting with President Roosevelt and Prime Minister Churchill. For several reasons, including major victories by Soviet troops, he dominated the meeting. Five months earlier he had met privately with Churchill in Moscow. At that time Churchill had scribbled a suggestion for a postwar "division of influence" (in effect a creation of satellite nations) in the Balkans to which Stalin had agreed. It also gave "90 percent to the Russians in Romania against 90 percent to the British in Greece. . . . 50–50 in Yugoslavia and Hungary, and 75 percent to Russia in Bulgaria." Churchill later recalled that "it was all settled in no more time than it takes to sit down." Now, at Yalta, Roosevelt "considered the European questions were so impossible that he wanted to stay out of them as far as practicable, except for the problems involving Germany."[10]

Roosevelt was quite ill, and his chief aide, Harry Hopkins, was suffering from a chronic blood disease. Both men would soon be dead. Churchill had the flu and was running a high fever. At Yalta, only Stalin was hale and hearty. His aims were to hold on to all the territory that had ever been under tsarist or Soviet rule, to extend Soviet influence as far west as possible so that the satellite nations of the USSR would provide a buffer zone against aggression from capitalist countries, to accomplish the same thing in Asia, and to collect massive reparations for the sufferings of the USSR in the war from Germany and from Germany's allies.

THE POLISH QUESTION

Stalin insisted on the partition of Germany to ensure that it would not be able to rebuild itself as a military power. Churchill, more afraid of Soviet aggression than of a remilitarized Germany, was opposed. Nevertheless, all three agreed on a protocol to take "such steps, including the disarmament, demilitarization and dismemberment of Germany as they [the Allies] deem requisite for future peace and security."[11]

The main issue at Yalta was Poland. It was the subject of seven out of the eight sessions, as well as of "nearly 18,000 words exchanged among the three leaders, in addition to lengthy discussions among their foreign ministers and other subordinates." It was not the boundaries of postwar Poland—these had been settled at Tehran—but rather the shape of the government that would rule Poland that was at issue. Roosevelt and Churchill wanted a genuinely independent and democratic government free of Soviet control. Stalin wanted "to keep as tight a grip on Poland as possible," and reminded the president and prime minister that Germany had twice used Poland as a corridor to invade his country, as had Napoleon.[12]

There was more than Poland at stake in these sessions. If Stalin could impose a Soviet-designed Communist government on Poland, then it followed that he could do it in the other nations his troops occupied. These included Hungary, Czechoslovakia, Romania, Bulgaria, Yugoslavia, possibly Austria, and East Germany.

Stalin cleverly managed to derail the Polish question by raising other issues. Primary among them was the organization of the United Nations. Stalin had at first insisted that each of the sixteen republics of the USSR have one vote in the General Assembly. Now, as part of the give-and-take involving Poland, he settled for three votes altogether. He also agreed that the Soviet Union would enter the war against Japan after Germany surrendered, with the understanding that certain strategic Japanese possessions would be taken over permanently by the Soviets. The Polish question was left hanging with a vague resolution that "democratic" leaders would be allowed to participate in free elections.[13] In effect, Stalin had won. After the war, Poland and most of the other countries of Eastern Europe would have Soviet-dominated Communist governments.

PUNISHING THE INNOCENT

As the talks at Yalta were proceeding, Soviet troops were securing the enemy areas they had captured. Their rage at the devastation that the Germans had wreaked on their homeland was fueled by Red Army propaganda. Posters and handbills announced "Red Army Soldier: You are now on German soil; the hour of revenge has struck!"[14]

The revenge was as inhumane and widespread as the horrors that provoked it. On a road in East Prussia, Russian tanks rolled over a column of fleeing German civilians, mostly women and children. They were squashed flat by the tanks, leaving behind a mass of dead bodies and screaming casualties. Other corpses lined the road. They had been shot in cold blood as target practice by soldiers being transported by trucks. Soviet flamethrowers indiscriminately destroyed homes, barns, and outbuildings. Civilians trying to escape across a frozen lake were strafed by Soviet warplanes. People were tortured, babies were killed, young girls were raped.

A survivor described events at a cow barn outside the town of Osterode. More than a hundred people had crowded into the barn in an effort to escape the Soviets. After a while, "soldiers came in, also officers, and fetched girls and young women. No shrieking, no begging, nothing helped. With revolvers in their hands, they gripped the women by their wrists and dragged them away. A father who wanted to protect his daughter was taken into the yard and shot. The girl was all the more the prey of these wild creatures."[15]

It was the same in Hungary, Romania, and parts of Yugoslavia and Czechoslovakia, but it was worst of all in Germany. The Red Army occupied West Prussia, East Prussia, and Pomerania. The German civilians occupying these areas were the ones who paid in the most horrible ways for the atrocities committed under the umbrella of Hitler's Scorched Earth Policy.

THE RACE TO THE CAPITAL

Neither Stalin, Zhukov, nor any of the other high-ranking Soviet military officers tried to curb the brutality of the Red Army. Indeed, a watchword of the troops was: "Stalin is with us!"[16] In any case, atrocities by Soviet soldiers were certainly not his main concern. His main concern was that the Americans and the British not outmaneuver him in gaining a postwar advantage in Europe, and particularly in Germany. On April 1, 1945, this concern narrowed down to who was going to take Berlin.

That day he received a telegram informing him that the Americans and British had come up with an "entirely feasible" plan to capture the city before the Soviets could, and that "preparations for its execution were in full swing."[17] Stalin immediately ordered Zhukov to plan an attack that would beat their allies to Berlin.

On April 12, while Zhukov was still deploying his forces, Stalin received the news that sixty-three-year-old President Franklin Roosevelt had died of a cerebral hemorrhage. Vice President Harry Truman had been sworn in to replace Roosevelt as president of the United States. Stalin instructed Beria to have the NKVD immediately compile a dossier on the man who would be his main adversary after the war.

Zhukov's forces moved into position on April 13. That same day Vienna, the capital city of Austria, fell to the Soviets. The street fighting had been vicious, and Soviet casualties had been high. It was a bloody preview of what was to follow in Berlin.

THE BATTLE OF BERLIN

More than 1.3 million soldiers of the Red Army attacked fortifications outside Berlin on the night of April 16. Their German opponents numbered approximately one million. However, only about three quarters of that force were trained soldiers. The rest were Hitler Youth, ranging from ten

On April 30, 1945, Russian soldiers fly their flag over the ruins of the Reichstag in Berlin.

to fifteen years of age, old men who had served as air-raid wardens or in the Home Guard, and housewives prepared to die for their city or their fatherland, if not necessarily for their Führer.

Hitler refused to face reality. He told his generals that "anyone who tells anyone else that the war is lost will be treated as a traitor, with all the consequences for him and his family—without regard to rank and prestige."[18] He demanded "a fight to the death and designated Berlin a fortress to be defended to the last."[19]

The Germans resisted fiercely. After the Soviets crossed the Oder River and fought their way through the suburbs to the city proper, the battle intensified. There was hand-to-hand fighting for each building. Each street thought to be secured was subjected to sniper fire and handmade bombs. Finally, on April 30, the Reichstag, the capitol building of the German government and once home to its parliament, was captured. When Soviet soldiers climbed to its roof and raised the hammer-and-sickle flag of the USSR, German resistance slowed to a halt.

In his bunker deep below the city streets of Berlin, on that same day, Adolf Hitler killed himself. By his orders, his body was burned and buried in a secret, unmarked grave. When Stalin heard the news, he remarked that it was "too bad it was impossible to take him alive."[20]

A week later, on May 7, 1945, Germany surrendered. Between 250,000 and 305,000 Red Army soldiers had died in the war's final battle for Berlin, but now the Soviet Union was at peace. In the cities, on the farms, and in the villages the Soviet people rejoiced. They didn't know that the Cold War was about to begin.

CHAPTER TEN

THE IRON CURTAIN DESCENDS

> A shadow has fallen upon the scenes so lately lighted by the Allied victory. Nobody knows what Soviet Russia and its Communist international organization intends to do in the immediate future, or what are the limits, if any, to their expansive and proselytizing tendencies. . . . From Stettin in the Baltic to Trieste in the Adriatic, an iron curtain has descended across the continent.
>
> Sir Winston Churchill's Cold War speech, Fulton, Missouri, March 5, 1946

Although America was still at war with Japan, the prospects for peace in Europe looked hopeful on June 26, 1945, when the United Nations (UN) was formally created in San Francisco. Germany had surrendered, and the Big Three—the United States, the Soviet Union, and Great Britain—still presented an image of cordial comradeship. Even as the UN delegates assembled, however, that image was being betrayed by the USSR.

In spite of the understanding that democratic Polish leaders would participate in a postwar Polish government, Stalin had established a puppet Communist regime controlled by Moscow. Under Beria, the NKVD had ferreted out "moderate politicians who had gone into hiding in Poland. They were all found and arrested."[1] So it was that six short weeks after the surrender of Germany, Poland became a Soviet satellite.

A FATEFUL TELEGRAM

The following month, the Potsdam Conference was held. It took place amid the luxury of unbombed villas in Potsdam, Germany, a swanky suburb of Berlin, and lasted from July 17 through August 2, 1945. The heads of government of the Soviet Union, the United States, and Great Britain attended along with numerous advisers, staff members, and other functionaries.

Shortly before the conference opened, Soviet Foreign Minister Molotov stopped off in Washington to pay his respects to the newly installed president, Harry Truman. The president responded with a cold and blunt condemnation of the Soviet actions in Poland. "I have never been talked to like that in my life," Molotov stuttered. "Carry out your agreements," Truman told him, "and you won't get talked to like that."[2]

The president had quite another matter on his mind the day before the conference opened. At seven-thirty P.M., on July 16, he received a telegram in Germany from Washington. "Operated on this morning," it said. "Diagnosis not yet complete but results seem satisfactory and already exceed expectations."[3] The meaning was clear to Truman. The first atomic bomb in the history of the world had been successfully detonated in the New Mexico desert.

ALLIES AT ODDS

British Prime Minister Winston Churchill also had other things on his mind that day. A general election was being held in Great Britain between his Conservative party and the Labour party of Clement Attlee. If the Conservatives won, Churchill would continue in office. If they lost, Attlee would become prime minister. Churchill had been immensely popular as a wartime leader, but now the war was over and the results of the election would not be known until midway through the Potsdam Conference.

In Churchill's opinion, Attlee and the Libourites did not appreciate the enormity of the Soviet threat to freedom and democracy in Europe. Only ten days after the German surrender, Churchill had discussed using air power for "striking at the communications of the Russian armies should they decide to advance farther than is agreed." He also approved the British keeping "approximately 700,000 German troops in essentially military formations in their zone" of occupied Germany. His strategy at Potsdam was to drive a diplomatic wedge between Truman and Stalin.[4]

Stalin, still afraid of flying, traveled to Potsdam by train. It was a thousand-mile journey, the first part through a Soviet Union ravaged by war. Stalin saw the fullness of the devastation firsthand. To leaders of the free world, except for Churchill, it had seemed unlikely that a nation so crushed would embark on further aggression. They didn't yet understand the extent to which Stalin was willing to sacrifice his own people.

Stalin's train had eleven cars, including four luxurious carriages that had once been the imperial quarters reserved for the tsar. All eleven cars were heavily guarded, and soldiers with machine guns rode atop the train. Shortly before he left Moscow, Stalin had suffered a heart attack. Nevertheless, once the conference began, he pursued his goals fiercely, showing no signs of illness or even weariness.

An immediate concern for Stalin on the eve of the Potsdam Conference was the effect on Soviet troops of the lifestyles and freedoms they were coming into contact with beyond the borders of their country. They were encountering capitalism in the form of the casual wealth of American soldiers trading wristwatches, silk stockings, and other items. They were being seduced by the democratic way of life. Incredible as it seems, Stalin jailed thousands upon thousands of returning Soviet soldiers because they had allegedly been contaminated by Western values. "They fear our friendship more than our enmity," was Churchill's accurate assessment of the Soviets.[5]

THE CHOICE

At this time the USSR had not yet entered the war against Japan. Just before the Potsdam Conference began, the Japanese sent a message to the Soviets asking them to act as intermediaries in negotiating surrender terms with the United States and Great Britain. The Soviets did not inform the United States and Britain of these peace feelers. Stalin did not want the war against Japan to end before the USSR could enter it and annex the territories agreed to at the Tehran meeting. However, U.S. Intelligence had intercepted the message and decoded it. The Japanese wanted the United States and Great Britain to stop insisting on "unconditional surrender."[6]

Stalin had promised Truman that the USSR would declare war on Japan no later than August 8. At the end of the first day of the Potsdam Conference, he spent the evening arranging for Soviet troop movements toward the Far East. He urged his generals to move with the greatest possible speed.

Both the Soviet Union and Great Britain had strategic goals in the Far East. These were not, however, the goals of President Truman and the United States. In a memo, Truman said there was a need to win the war "before too many of our allies are committed there and have made substantial contributions toward the defeat of Japan."[7]

There were several ways Truman could accomplish this. He could drop the demand for unconditional surrender, he could launch a high-casualty invasion of the Japanese Islands, he could simply wait and starve the Japanese into defeat, or he could drop the atomic bomb on Japan. If he agreed to negotiate the conditions of surrender, he would be accused of appeasement toward an enemy that had destroyed an American fleet at Pearl Harbor before declaring war. If he dropped the bomb, it would finish Japan and succeed in "making the Russians more manageable in Europe."[8]

MEETING STALIN'S DEMANDS

At Potsdam, on July 18, Truman told Churchill about the successful atomic bomb test. He informed him that there were bombs ready to be dropped on Japan if that was necessary. They discussed telling Stalin. "I had best just tell him after one of our meetings," said Truman, "that we have an entirely novel form of bomb . . . which we think will have decisive effects upon the Japanese will to continue the war." Churchill agreed.[9]

Truman did not tell Stalin immediately. He bided his time. There were other matters to be resolved. As Stalin pressed for ships and other aid from the United States so that the Soviet Union could effectively join the war against Japan, and Truman hedged, the dictator switched topics and pushed both the president and Churchill into a corner. He demanded that the Soviets be given one third of the captured German navy. It had been seized mostly by the British, but in the spirit of give-and-take, Stalin's demand was met.

For Stalin, much of the negotiations were not so much a matter of give-and-take, however, as of persuading Truman and Churchill to accept as permanent that which had already been put in place by the Soviet armies. He argued that during the war, as the Red Army liberated both enemy and friendly countries, they had naturally set up friendly governments to protect their rear. Now, as Stalin pulled his armies back, he wanted the United States and Great Britain to recognize those governments as legitimate. What he didn't say was that those countries would then provide a buffer zone between the Soviet Union and the West. Truman and Churchill understood this, but could not deny that the puppet governments were in place and functioning.

The sticking point was East Germany. As the Soviet army had advanced through Germany toward Berlin, Stalin and Beria's NKVD had seen to it that millions of Poles moved into the easternmost border areas of Germany. This was part of the agreement by which the Soviet Union took land from Poland and Poland was granted that German territory. However, Stalin was now carrying it a step further. He pointed out that "it is very hard to restore the German administration" in what was now the Soviet-occupied nation of East Germany itself because "everyone has run away."[10] Stalin added that Germans who returned to East Germany would be hanged. Finally, it was decided that the fate of East Germany would be decided as part of an overall agreement on the reparations the Germans must pay for the damages they had caused in the war.

STALIN'S NUCLEAR POKER FACE

At seven-thirty P.M. on July 24, 1945, at Potsdam, there occurred the "turning point in history," which Professor Charles L. Mee Jr. identifies as the moment when "the twentieth century's nuclear arms race began."[11] Truman described the moment in his memoirs: "I casually mentioned to Stalin that we had a new weapon of unusual destructive force. All he said was that he was glad to hear it and hoped we would make 'good use of it against the Japanese.'"[12] Truman recalled that "the Russian premier showed no special interest."[13]

Truman did not identify the weapon as atomic, or nuclear. Stalin didn't ask what kind of weapon it was. He didn't ask for details about its development. He didn't complain about not having been informed about it previously. He didn't request that the technology involved be shared with Soviet scientists. He simply didn't appear to be very interested in the Americans' new weapon.

Of course it was an act. The Soviets had been engaged in nuclear research for the previous three years. They had a spy, a German-born physicist named Klaus Fuchs, at Los Alamos, New Mexico, while the bomb was being developed. He had passed on America's atomic secrets to scientists in the Soviet Union, and they had pronounced his information "extremely excellent and very valuable." Stalin understood thoroughly what Truman told him, and he knew exactly how important the news was. He immediately instructed Molotov to telegraph scientists working on the Soviet atomic project "to hurry up the work." Then Stalin himself cabled Beria, who was in charge of the project, to "put on the pressure."[14]

CHURCHILL'S DEFEAT

Churchill believed that Truman had successfully misled Stalin as to the enormity of the importance of the atomic bomb. Nevertheless, he was very depressed when he awoke the next morning. He was about to leave Potsdam for London to be there when the results of the election for prime minister were announced. "Perhaps this is the end," he sighed.[15]

Stalin thought otherwise. According to Churchill, Stalin told him that "all his information from Communist and other sources confirmed his belief that I should be returned by a majority of about eighty" seats in the British parliament.[16] Stalin himself preferred dealing with a conservative British government to negotiating with a Labour party regime. He had a deep distrust of left-wing governments not under the thumb of the Kremlin.

On July 26, in London, Churchill learned that the Labour party had won and that Clement Attlee had replaced him as prime minister. When the news reached Potsdam, Stalin became ill and was temporarily unable to attend the conference meetings. Molotov was also shocked. He couldn't understand how the candidates "could not tell what would be the result."[17] The Soviet leadership took it for granted that since Churchill had been in power, he would have seen to it that the election was rigged.

AVOIDING DECISIONS

Two days after winning the election, Prime Minister Clement Attlee arrived in Potsdam. By then, another message from the Japanese to the Russians had been intercepted by American Intelligence. Japan offered to surrender unconditionally with the sole provision that it be allowed to retain its emperor. It was a question of Japanese national "existence and honor."[18] When Stalin passed on the message to Truman, who already knew of it, the offer was rejected.

By now Truman was studying maps of Japan to decide on possible targets for the atomic bomb. He had issued a Potsdam Declaration, agreed to by Attlee, assuring the Japanese people that they would not be "enslaved as a race or destroyed as a nation" if Japan surrendered. However, the final paragraph still called for "unconditional surrender."[19] It had originally called for a "constitutional monarchy under the present dynasty," but Truman took that wording out before releasing the Declaration.[20] The Japanese read the Potsdam Declaration as nothing but a restating of the same old U.S. position.

After Attlee arrived, and Stalin felt well enough to attend, the Potsdam Conference drew to a close. As far as Europe was concerned, not many of the diplomatic aims of the United States and Great Britain had been accomplished. Stalin had been granted one third of Germany's merchant ships, as well as its navy. He had gained the right to collect reparations from enemy zones occupied by the Red Army, including those in Germany, Austria, Hungary, Romania, and Bulgaria. The Soviet Union would also receive a portion of reparations (to be determined at a later date) from enemy territories occupied by the United States and Great Britain. Many of the thornier questions concerning the puppet governments set up by the Red Army in enemy countries, the fate of East Germany, the Polish bor-

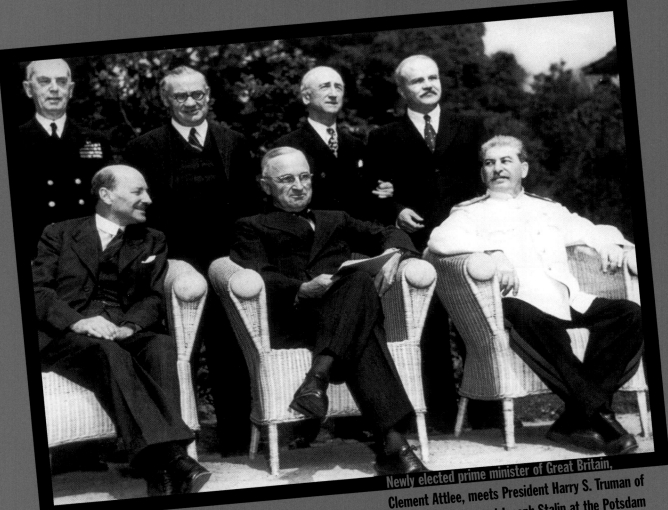

Newly elected prime minister of Great Britain, Clement Attlee, meets President Harry S. Truman of the United States and Joseph Stalin at the Potsdam Conference in August 1945.

ders, and others, were put on hold. A Council of Foreign Ministers was to be set up "to handle questions too difficult for settlement at Potsdam."[21]

Putting the questions on hold made it possible for Stalin to later firm up the Soviet grip on the governments of the nations of Eastern Europe, including East Germany. This was the area that would form a buffer zone between the Soviet Union and the West. It would be behind the Iron Curtain defined by Winston Churchill. It would be the area, during the decades that followed, where some of the hottest battles of the Cold War would be fought.

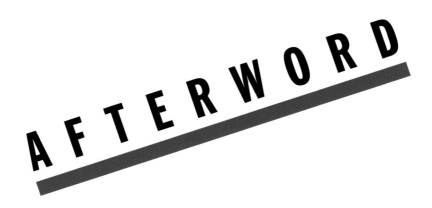

AFTERWORD

On August 2, Stalin, Attlee, and Truman left Potsdam. The conference had confirmed Stalin as "the main victor in the war so far as expansion of territory and influence in Europe was concerned."[1] Neither Churchill nor Attlee had succeeded in reestablishing British influence over the continent. Truman, however, had made the one decision at Potsdam that would most influence the future of Europe, particularly the Soviet Union, and the world. Three days before leaving Potsdam, Truman issued the order to drop the atomic bomb on Japan. His coded message to the War Department read: "Suggestion approved. Release when ready but not sooner than August 2," the day the Potsdam Conference was to end.[2]

American military leaders by now had been consulted about dropping the bomb. General Dwight Eisenhower, Admiral William Leahy, General Curtis LeMay, General Hap Arnold, Admiral Ernest King, and others thought it was not necessary. In Eisenhower's opinion, "the Japanese were ready to surrender and it wasn't necessary to hit them with that awful thing."[3] General Douglas MacArthur, the supreme commander of American forces in the Pacific, was not consulted, but after the war he said that he too thought it was not necessary to drop the atomic bomb.

The ultimate responsibility was of course Truman's, and he did not hesitate to accept it. He freely admitted that "the final decision of where and when to use the atomic bomb was up to me. Let there be no mistake about it. I regarded the bomb as a military weapon and never had any doubt that it should be used." He said that once he had made the decision to drop the atomic bomb, he "went to bed and slept soundly."[4]

The first atomic bomb was dropped on Hiroshima by the flying fortress *Enola Gay* at nine-fifteen A.M. on Monday, August 6, 1945. One hundred thousand people were killed immediately. Subsequently another 100,000 died from the atomic radiation loosed by the bomb. Three days later a second bomb was dropped on Nagasaki. There an initial death toll of 70,000 eventually mounted to 140,000. Nonlethal effects of the bombs would be suffered by the people of the two cities over the following decades.

On August 8, two days after the first atomic bomb was dropped, the Soviet Union declared war on Japan. A week later, on August 14, Japan surrendered to Great Britain and the United States. On September 2, the Japanese signed official surrender documents aboard the U.S. battleship *Missouri*. Although the surrender was unconditional, the previously rejected Japanese plea that they be allowed to keep their emperor was now honored.

Stalin vigorously pursued the war against the Japanese for four weeks until shortly after the surrender papers were signed aboard the *Missouri*. During that time, according to the Soviets, more than 8,000 of their soldiers were killed and more than 22,000 were wounded. The casualties bought Stalin the foothold he wanted in the Far East. The Red Army had taken over the strategically important Manchurian railway system. They "were able to complete the occupation of central Manchuria, capture Port Arthur, and secure the northern half of Korea."[5] The Communist government they set up in North Korea would prove a threat to the United States right up to the present day.

In effect, the brief Russian campaign against Japan was one of the steps leading to the Cold War. The inability to reach agreement on democratic governments for Soviet satellite countries at Potsdam was another of those steps. Some historians believe that the dropping of the atomic bombs on Hiroshima and Nagasaki was the third, and perhaps the most decisive, step. The extent of the damage prompted Stalin to promise unlimited funds to develop a Soviet A-bomb. A team of Russian and captive German scientists was placed under the supervision of Beria and the NKVD with orders to work with all possible speed. When the most prominent of them, the physicist Peter Kapitsa, refused to work on the military uses of nuclear energy, he was imprisoned.

To the surprise of American scientists who had predicted it would take much longer, it took only four years for the Russians to develop an atomic bomb. On September 23, 1949, President Truman told his cabinet that "we have evidence that within recent weeks an atomic explosion occurred in the U.S.S.R."[6] With that announcement, the Cold War threat went nuclear. The United States and the Soviet Union began stockpiling nuclear weapons. For the next forty years, communism and democracy would be poised to wipe each other out. The ever-present danger of the Cold War would be the danger of mass destruction.

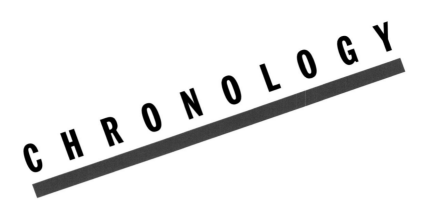

CHRONOLOGY

1939 — August — Soviet Union signs nonaggression pact with Nazi Germany.
September — Germany and Soviet Union invade Poland.
November — Winter War begins with Soviet invasion of Finland.

1940 — March — Winter War ends and Finland cedes strategic territory to Soviet Union.
Summer — Katyn Forest massacre of Polish soldiers by NKVD under Beria's command.

1941 — June 22 — Operation Barbarossa, the Nazi invasion of Soviet Union, is launched.
August — Stalin issues Order 270 labeling Soviet POWs traitors and punishing their families.
September — German army reaches outskirts of Leningrad and siege begins; Germans and Ukrainians massacre 33,000 Jews at Babi Yar.
October-November — German army advances on Moscow; government is evacuated; populace panics.
December — Japanese attack Pearl Harbor; United States declares war on Japan and Germany.

1941–42 — Winter — Severe winter blizzards and General Zhukov's defense strategy prevent Germans from taking Moscow.

1942 — January — Road of Life built across frozen Lake Ladoga brings relief supplies to Leningrad.

May—Stalin creates Central Staff for Partisan Warfare utilizing NKVD for surveillance of guerrilla fighters; Soviet Foreign Minister Vyacheslav Molotov meets with U.S. President Franklin Roosevelt, who promises second front in Europe in 1942.

August—First face-to-face meeting between British Prime Minister Winston Churchill and Stalin.

Summer—Germans mount massive offensive against Stalingrad.

1943— January—Red Army recaptures Stalingrad from the Germans; Soviets partially succeed in lifting the siege of Leningrad.

July—The Battle of Kursk, most massive tank battle ever fought, ends with Soviet victory.

September—Hitler authorizes retreat of German army and the Scorched Earth Policy, destroying all it leaves behind.

November—U.S. President Roosevelt, British Prime Minister Winston Churchill, and Soviet Premier Joseph Stalin meet in Tehran, Iran, to discuss second front and postwar arrangements.

1944— January—After nine hundred days, the siege of Leningrad ends.

February—NKVD troops deport Chechens to Siberia, slaughter those who refuse to go.

June—D Day landings of U.S. and British troops on Normandy beaches open second front in France.

July-August—Soviet troops pursue Germans across Polish border; atrocities mark German suppression of rebellion in Warsaw.

December—Massive German counteroffensive results in Battle of the Bulge; American forces are pinned down in Ardennes forest, Belgium.

1945— January—Stalin orders all-out Soviet attack on Germans to relieve pressure on Americans trapped in the Ardennes.

February—Stalin, Roosevelt, and Churchill meet at Yalta; agreements are reached affecting nations involved in European conflict.

April—U.S. President Franklin Roosevelt dies of a cerebral hemorrhage; the Red Army launches an attack on Berlin; Adolf Hitler commits suicide as Soviet troops capture Berlin.

May 7—Germany surrenders.

June—United Nations formally created in San Francisco.

July 16—First atomic bomb successfully detonated in New Mexico desert.

July 24—Truman informs Stalin that United States has powerful new weapon without mentioning atomic or nuclear nature.

July—Potsdam Declaration reiterating call for unconditional surrender is released and rejected by Japanese.

July-August—New U.S. president Harry Truman, Churchill, and Stalin meet at Potsdam, Germany; during the conference, Churchill is voted out of office and replaced by new British prime minister Clement Attlee; discussions do not resolve many key questions regarding postwar Europe.

August 6—First atomic bomb is dropped on Hiroshima, Japan.

August 8—The Soviet Union declares war on Japan.

August 9—Second atomic bomb is dropped on Nagasaki, Japan.

August 14—Japan surrenders to the United States and Great Britain.

September 2—Japanese sign official surrender documents aboard the U.S. battleship *Missouri*.

September—War between Soviet Union and Japan ends.

1949— September 23—President Truman tells his cabinet he has learned that the Soviet Union has successfully tested an atomic bomb.

CHAPTER NOTES

PREFACE

1. Walter Laqueur, *Stalin: The Glasnost Revelations* (New York: Charles Scribner's Sons, 1990), pp. 216, 218.
2. Geoffrey Hosking, *The First Socialist Society: A History of the Soviet Union From Within* (Cambridge, MA: Harvard University Press, 1996), p. 296.

CHAPTER ONE

Opening quote: Harrison Salisbury, *The 900 Days: The Siege of Leningrad* (New York: Harper & Row, 1969), p. 78.

1. *Encyclopaedia Britannica,* vol. 10 (Chicago: Encyclopaedia Britannica, Inc., 1984), p. 797.
2. Gabriel Gorodetsky, *Grand Illusion: Stalin and the German Invasion of Russia* (New Haven, CT: Yale University Press, 1999), pp. 130–131.
3. Salisbury, p. 61.
4. Alan Bullock, *Hitler and Stalin: Parallel Lives* (New York: Alfred A. Knopf, 1992), p. 717.
5. Bullock, p. 705.
6. Bullock, p. 719.
7. Bullock, p. 721.
8. Gorodetsky, p. 115.
9. Michael J. Lyons, *World War II: A Short History* (Upper Saddle River, NJ: Prentice Hall, 1999). p. 117.

CHAPTER TWO

Opening quote: Walter Laqueur, *Stalin: The Glasnost Revelations* (New York: Charles Scribner's Sons, 1990), p. 218.

1. Michael J. Lyons, *World War II: A Short History* (Upper Saddle River, NJ: Prentice Hall, 1999), p. 121.
2. Lyons, p.121.
3. Laqueur, p. 218.
4. Laqueur, p. 218.
5. Laqueur, p. 215.
6. *Encyclopaedia Britannica*, vol. 2 (Chicago: Encyclopaedia Britannica, Inc., 1984), p. 790.
7. Author uncredited. *Lavrenti Beria* (New York Public Library Electronic Resources: Biography Resource Center, *Encyclopedia of World Biography*, Gale Research, 1998), p. 2.
8. William L. Shirer, *The Rise and Fall of the Third Reich: A History of Nazi Germany* (New York: Simon & Schuster, 1960), p. 956.
9. Laqueur, p. 217.
10. Laqueur, p. 220.
11. Lyons, p. 119.
12. Lyons, p. 121.

CHAPTER THREE

Opening quote: Harrison Salisbury, *The 900 Days: The Siege of Leningrad* (New York: Harper & Row, 1969), p. 468.
1. Richard Overy, *Russia's War: Blood Upon the Snow* (New York: Penguin Putnam, 1997), p. 140.
2. Overy, p. 135.
3. Overy, p. 132.
4. Overy, p. 138.
5. Overy, p. 142.

CHAPTER FOUR

Opening quote: Dmitri Volkogonov, *Stalin: Triumph & Tragedy* (New York: Grove Weidenfeld, 1991), p. 436.
1. H. Montgomery Hyde, *Stalin: The History of a Dictator* (New York: Da Capo Press, 1971), p. 459.
2. Hyde, p. 459.
3. Alan Bullock, *Hitler and Stalin: Parallel Lives* (New York: Alfred A. Knopf, 1992), p. 734.
4. Ronald Hingley, *Joseph Stalin: Man and Legend* (New York: McGraw-Hill, 1974), p. 323.
5. Hyde, p. 460.
6. Richard Overy, *Russia's War: Blood Upon the Snow* (New York: Penguin Putnam, 1997), p. 191.

7. Hyde, p. 460.
8. Michael J. Lyons, *World War II: A Short History* (Upper Saddle River, NJ: Prentice Hall, 1999), p. 123.
9. Hyde, p. 448.
10. Hyde, p. 448.
11. Hyde, p. 447.
12. Overy, p. 151.
13. Lyons, p. 123.
14. *Chronicle of the 20th Century* (Mount Kisco, NY: Chronicle Publications, 1987), p. 530.

CHAPTER FIVE

Opening quote: Richard Overy, *Russia's War: Blood Upon the Snow* (New York: Penguin Putnam, 1997), p. 204.
1. Overy, p. 181.
2. Georgi K. Zhukov, *Marshal Zhukov's Greatest Battles* (New York: Harper & Row, 1969), p. 156.
3. Ted Gottfried, *Nazi Germany: The Face of Tyranny* (Brookfield, CT: Twenty-First Century Books, 2000), pp. 89–90.

CHAPTER SIX

Opening quote: Georgi K. Zhukov, *Marshal Zhukov's Greatest Battles* (New York: Harper & Row, 1969), p. 191.
1. Ronald Hingley, *Joseph Stalin: Man and Legend* (New York: McGraw-Hill, 1974), p. 338.
2. Richard Overy, *Russia's War: Blood Upon the Snow* (New York: Penguin Putnam, 1997), p. 191.
3. Author uncredited. *Vyacheslav Mikhailovich Molotov* (New York Public Library Electronic Resources: Biography Resource Center, *Encyclopedia of World Biography*, Gale Research, 1999), p. 1.
4. Author uncredited. *Vyacheslav Mikhailovich Molotov* (New York Public Library Electronic Resources: Biography Resource Center, *Contemporary Newsmakers*, Gale Research, 1988), p. 2.
5. Chris Ward, *Stalin's Russia* (New York: Oxford University Press, 1999), p. 202.
6. Walter Laqueur, *Stalin: The Glastnost Revelations* (New York: Charles Scribner's Sons, 1990), pp. 220–221.
7. Laqueur, p. 222.
8. Alan Bullock, *Hitler and Stalin: Parallel Lives* (New York: Alfred A. Knopf, 1992), p. 785.
9. Bullock, p. 786.
10. Bullock, p. 785.
11. Bullock, p. 786.
12. Bullock, p. 786.

13. Hingley, pp. 333–334.
14. Bullock, p. 786.
15. Ward, p. 192.
16. Bullock, p. 782.
17. William Craig, *Enemy at the Gates* (New York: Penguin Books, 2000), p. 363.
18. Craig, p. 200.
19. Craig, p. 205.
20. Craig, p. 243.
21. Earl F. Ziemke and the editors of Time-Life Books, *The Soviet Juggernaut* (Alexandria, VA: Time-Life Books, 1980), p. 21.

CHAPTER SEVEN

Opening quote: Harrison Salisbury, *The 900 Days: The Siege of Leningrad* (New York: Harper & Row, 1969), p. 550.
1. Salisbury, p. 543.
2. Salisbury, p. 508.
3. Salisbury, p. 509.
4. Salisbury, p. 549.
5. Earl F. Ziemke and the editors of Time-Life Books, *The Soviet Juggernaut* (Alexandria, VA: Time-Life Books Inc., 1980), p. 30.
6. Richard Overy, *Russia's War: Blood Upon the Snow* (New York: Penguin Putnam, 1997), p. 241.
7. Overy, p. 241.
8. Ziemke, p. 33.
9. Ziemke, p. 36.
10. Ziemke, p. 39.
11. Ziemke, p. 37.
12. Ziemke, p. 38.
13. Georgi K. Zhukov, *Marshal Zhukov's Greatest Battles* (New York: Harper & Row, 1969), p. 255.
14. Salisbury, p. 562.

CHAPTER EIGHT

Opening quote: William Tecumseh Sherman, *1879 Graduation Address at Michigan Military Academy* in *Bartlett's Familiar Quotations: Fourteenth Edition* (Boston: Little, Brown and Company, 1968), p. 705a.
1. Earl F. Ziemke and the editors of Time-Life Books, *The Soviet Juggernaut* (Alexandria, VA: Time-Life Books, 1980), p. 78.
2. Dmitri Volkogonov, *Stalin: Triumph & Tragedy* (New York: Grove Weidenfeld, 1991), p. 488.

3. *Chronicle of the 20th Century* (Mount Kisco, NY: Chronicle Publications, 1987), p. 558.

4. Richard Overy, *Russia's War: Blood Upon the Snow* (New York: Penguin Putnam, 1997), p. 282.

5. Overy, pp. 282–283.

6. Overy, p. 291.

7. Overy, p. 296.

8. W. H. Auden, *Selected Poems* (New York: Vintage International, 1989), p. 86.

CHAPTER NINE

Opening quote: Richard Overy, *Russia's War: Blood Upon the Snow* (New York: Penguin Putnam, 1997), p. 310.

1. Harrison Salisbury, *The 900 Days: The Siege of Leningrad* (New York: Harper & Row, 1969), p. 575.

2. Earl F. Ziemke and the editors of Time-Life Books, *The Soviet Juggernaut* (Alexandria, VA: Time-Life Books, 1980), p. 192.

3. Ziemke, p. 192.

4. Ziemke, p. 195.

5. Ziemke, p. 178.

6. Stephen E. Ambrose, *Citizen Soldiers: June 7, 1944–May 7, 1945* (New York: Simon & Schuster, 1997), p. 185.

7. Ambrose, p. 184.

8. H. Montgomery Hyde, *Stalin: The History of a Dictator* (New York: Da Capo Press, 1971), p. 514.

9. Ziemke, p. 180.

10. Alan Bullock, *Hitler and Stalin: Parallel Lives* (New York: Alfred A. Knopf, 1992), pp. 870–871.

11. Bullock, p. 872.

12. Bullock, p. 873.

13. Bullock, p. 874.

14. Ziemke, p. 188.

15. Ziemke, p. 188.

16. Hyde, p. 482.

17. Hyde, p. 524.

18. Bullock, p. 877.

19. Author uncredited, *The Battle for Berlin*, Internet: <www.zhukov.org/Berlin.htm>

20. *The Battle for Berlin*

CHAPTER TEN

Opening quote: Charles L. Mee Jr., *Meeting at Potsdam* (New York: Franklin Square Press, 1975), p. 240.

1. *Chronicle of the 20th Century* (Mount Kisco, NY: Chronicle Publications, 1987), p. 595.
2. Mee, p. 13.
3. David McCullough, *Truman* (New York: Simon & Schuster, 1992), p. 416.
4. Mee, pp. 28–29.
5. Mee, p. 45.
6. Mee, p. 17.
7. Mee, p. 60.
8. Mee, p. 60.
9. Mee, p. 86.
10. Mee, p. 126.
11. Mee, p. 174.
12. McCullough, p. 442.
13. Mee, p. 173.
14. McCullough, p. 443.
15. Mee, p. 175.
16. Mee, p. 91.
17. Ronald Hingley, *Joseph Stalin: Man and Legend* (New York: McGraw-Hill, 1974), p. 365.
18. Mee, p. 183.
19. McCullough, p. 447.
20. Ted Gottfried, *Enrico Fermi: Pioneer of the Atomic Age* (New York: Facts on File, 1992), p. 103.
21. *Encyclopaedia Britannica,* vol. 19 (Chicago: Encyclopaedia Britannica, 1984), p. 1012.

AFTERWORD . . .

1. Ronald Hingley, *Joseph Stalin: Man and Legend* (New York: McGraw-Hill, 1974), p. 366.
2. David McCullough, *Truman* (New York: Simon & Schuster, 1992), p. 448.
3. Ted Gottfried, *Enrico Fermi: Pioneer of the Atomic Age* (New York: Facts on File, 1992), p. 105.
4. McCullough, pp. 442–443.
5. Alan Bullock, *Hitler and Stalin: Parallel Lives* (New York: Alfred A. Knopf, 1992), p. 904.
6. *Chronicle of the 20th Century* (Mount Kisco, NY: Chronicle Publications, 1987), p. 667.

GLOSSARY

Battle of the Bulge—massive winter surprise attack by Germans on American troops in Belgium

Big Three—wartime term referring to the leaders of the United States, Soviet Union, and Great Britain

Bolsheviks—early name for Communists

booby trap—hidden explosive designed to blow up unexpectedly

buffer zone—territories or nations forming a protective area between potentially hostile countries

Central Staff for Partisan Warfare—organization to centralize government control over guerrilla groups

Chechens—citizens of Chechnya, mostly Muslims with their own language and traditions, who were exiled in great numbers to Siberia during the war

Cold War—period between the end of World War II and the collapse of the Soviet Union marked by aggression and threats of aggression between the USSR and the free nations of the world

collaborators—Soviet citizens, mostly non-Russians, who fought alongside or otherwise aided the Germans, in the war against the USSR

commissar—head of any of the departments in the local or national governments of the USSR

communism—ownership of all property by the community as a whole

Cossacks—military tribesmen who originally served the tsar and gained a reputation for staging pogroms; a quarter million Cossacks fought for the Germans during the Great Fatherland War

Crimea—agricultural and industrial region of the Ukraine rich in wheat and iron ore.

cult of personality—identification of the nation and people with leader

D Day—June 6, 1944, the day American and British troops landed in Normandy to open a second front in France

demilitarization—dismantling of armies, navies, and air forces

dysentery—disease of the intestines characterized by extreme diarrhea

Führer (leader)—Adolf Hitler's title

Great Fatherland War—name given to World War II by Soviet citizens

gulag—primitive prison camp usually set in a remote area

hedgehog formation—troops surrounding supply depots to form isolated defensive strong points

Hitler Youth—organization to indoctrinate German youth with Nazi dogma

Home Guard—overage or underage Germans drafted to defend their immediate areas

Ice Road—road across frozen Lake Ladoga and beyond, which was used to deliver food and supplies to Leningrad during the siege

Iron Curtain—Winston Churchill's phrase defining the line across Europe behind which dictatorship, secrecy, and lack of freedom characterized Soviet satellite nations

Lend Lease—U.S. program supplying war material to the USSR and other allies in World War II

Leningrad—former Russian capital city; originally St. Petersburg, then Petrograd, now again called St. Petersburg

Leningrad Renaissance—the rebuilding of Leningrad after the siege was ended

Luftwaffe—German air force

Metropolitan—regional leader of the Russian Orthodox Church

Molotov cocktail—bottles filled with gasoline and hurled as bombs

NKVD—Soviet secret police

Operation Barbarossa—June 1941 invasion of the Soviet Union by Nazi Germany

Operation Blue—German campaign to take Stalingrad and gain control of the route to Soviet oil fields

Operation Typhoon—German campaign to take Moscow

Panther—lightweight German tank; highly maneuverable but very vulnerable

partisans—bands of guerrilla fighters operating behind enemy lines

partition—separating a country into two parts with two separate governments, as was the case with East and West Germany following World War II

Patriarch—national leader of the Russian Orthodox Church

Pavlov's House—strategic landmark in the heart of Stalingrad from which soldiers fought against overwhelming odds and held off the Germans for fifty-eight days

peasant—farm laborer

pincer movement—military tactic in which two armies approach the enemy from different directions and then come together to attack from both sides

pogrom—raids in which Jews were robbed, raped, and murdered

Politburo—five-member panel appointed by the Central Committee of the Communist party to make quick decisions in urgent matters

preemptive offensive—attack on the enemy intended to head off an enemy attack

Provisional Government—body that ruled Russia between abdication of Tsar Nicholas II and the Bolshevik takeover

purge—dispensing with political foes by exile, imprisonment, or execution

Red Army—military land forces of the Soviet Union

reparations—payment to a government or an individual for damages suffered by the acts of an aggressor nation

Road of Life—another name for the Ice Road used to supply Leningrad under siege

Russian Social Democratic Labour party—organization that evolved into the Communist party

satellite nations— countries whose policies are determined by another country, as in the case of Poland at the end of World War II

Schutzmannschaften—Ukrainian battalions organized by the Nazis to hunt down and kill Jews

Scorched Earth Policy—Hitler's policy ordering the retreating German army to destroy everything it left behind

second front—attack on mainland Europe by the United States and Great Britain to take pressure off the Soviets

siege—prolonged military encirclement of a city to force its surrender by denying it food and supplies, and preventing suffering citizens from leaving

stalemate—the point at which a battle, or series of battles, results in a standoff without a victory

Stalinism—a redefining of communism into brutal one-man rule serving the power hunger of Joseph Stalin

State Defense Committee (GKO)—five members of the Politburo with Stalin as chairman, which directed all aspects of the war effort against Germany

Stavka—Soviet supreme command charged with seeing that the Red Army general staff carried out the orders of the GKO

Tiger—heavily armored German tank; impervious to mortar fire but not very maneuverable

trackwolf—German railroad device, which tore up crossties as it rolled along the tracks

Ukraine—non-Russian Soviet republic of farmlands and mineral resources

unconditional surrender—terms agreed upon by the United States, Great Britain, and the USSR for ending the war with Germany and Japan

Union of Soviet Socialist Republics (USSR)—collection of nations making up the Soviet Union

untermenschen—Jews, Slavs, and all others considered by Nazis to be ethnically inferior to Germans

Wehrmacht—the German army

Whites—anti-Communist subjects of tsarist Russia

Winter War—1939–1940 conflict between the Soviet Union and Finland

Zitadelle (Citadel)—German code name for the Battle of Kursk, the greatest tank battle ever fought

FOR MORE INFORMATION

Bullock, Alan. *Hitler and Stalin: Parallel Lives*. New York: Alfred A. Knopf, 1992.

Hosking, Geoffrey. *Russia and the Russians: A History*. Boston: Harvard University Press, 2001.

MacKenzie, David. *A History of Russia and the Soviet Union*. Homewood, IL: Dorset Press, 1977.

Matthews, John R. *The Rise and Fall of the Soviet Union*. San Diego, CA: Lucent Books, 2000.

McCullough, David. *Truman*. New York: Simon & Schuster, 1992.

Mee, Charles L., Jr. *Meeting at Potsdam*. New York: Franklin Square Press, 1975.

Overy, Richard. *Russia's War: Blood Upon the Snow*. New York: Penguin Putnam, 1997.

Salisbury, Harrison. *The 900 Days: The Siege of Leningrad*. New York: Harper & Row, 1969.

Shirer, William L. *The Rise and Fall of the Third Reich: A History of Nazi Germany*. New York: Simon & Schuster, 1960.

Volkogonov, Dmitri. *Stalin: Triumph & Tragedy*. New York: Grove Weidenfeld, 1988.

Ward, Chris. *Stalin's Russia*. New York: Oxford University Press, 1999.

Zhukov, Georgi K. *Marshal Zhukov's Greatest Battles.* New York: Harper & Row, 1969.

Ziemke, Earl F., and the editors of Time-Life Books. *The Soviet Juggernaut.* Alexandria, VA: Time-Life Books, 1980.

INTERNET SITES

History of St. Petersburg: 900-Day Siege of Leningrad
<www.cityvision2000.com/history/900days.htm>

Joseph Stalin Reference Archive: 1879–1953
<http://www.marxists.org/reference/archive/stalin/>

Chronology of the Holocaust 1939–1941
June 22, 1941: "Operation Barbarossa"
<http://212.143.122.31/about_holocaust/chronology/1939-1941-/1941/chronology_1941_9.html>

Stalingrad: All you want to know about the great battle

The Battle of Kursk
<http://web.mitsi.com/zhukov.kursk.htm>

INDEX